Beyond Religion Two

A few excerpts from 5 STAR reviews on Amazon for

BEYOND RELIGION II

..."Beyond Religion II" is the kind of book that expands your mind, gets you thinking, leaves you questioning the simple truths of life and manages to put a smile on your face all the while.

L. Collins TOP 1000 REVIEWER, USA

...Mr. Kapuscinski's enormous base of religious, scientific, and mythological knowledge makes this a truly enlightening read. And as always, the author's wit and humor in the text make it constantly enjoyable.

Ronald Piecuch USA

...Stanislaw Kapuscinski's (aka Stan I. S. Law) "Beyond Religion II" is a collection of essays that investigates the nature of truth. ...Recommended to anyone who wants an open-minded, unbiased investigation of the nature of truth and reality!

J. Linson, USA

... Another reviewer says it better than I ever could: "The essays are deep yet light, profound yet presented without philosophical mumbo-jumbo."

Ron Pike USA

...Mr. Kapuscinski's style, with a constant blend of wit and humor, remains a pleasure to read. ...Mr. Kapuscinski never gets "preachy", simply presenting the information for the audience to consume.

Donna A. Piecuch

Birds of Paradise? Wunderkind? Antichrist? Bliss? ...and forty-eight others. All esoteric, seemingly weird, puzzling, peculiar... full of fun!

Anetta Bach

Other books by Stanislaw Kapuscinski

DICTIONARY OF BIBLICAL SYMBOLISM
KEY TO IMMORTALITY
DELUSIONS—Pragmatic Realism
VISULIZATION—Creating your own Universe
BEYOND RELIGION Volumes I
BEYOND RELIGION Volumes III
[Three Collections of Essays on Perception of Reality]

Fiction by Stan I.S. Law
(aka **Stanislaw Kapuscinski**)

Novels

WALL—Love, Sex, and Immortality [Aquarius Trilogy Book One]
PLUTO EFFECT [Aquarius Trilogy Book Two]
OLYMPUS—Of Gods and Men [Aquarius Trilogy Book Three]
YESHUA—Missing Years of Jesus
PETER AND PAUL—Intuitive Sequel to Yeshûa
MARVIN CLARK—In Search of Freedom
GIFT OF GAMMAN
ENIGMA OF THE SECOND COMING
ONE JUST MAN [Winston Trilogy Book One]
ELOHIM [Winston Trilogy Book Two]
WINSTON'S KINGDOM [Winston Trilogy Book Three]
THE PRINCESS
GATE—Things my Mother told Me
ALEC [Alexander Trilogy Book One]
ALEXANDER [Alexander Trilogy Book Two]
SACHA—THE WAY BACK [Alexander Trilogy Book Three]
THE AVATAR SYNDROME [Prequel to the Headless World]
HEADLESS WORLD [Sequel to the Avatar Syndrome]
NOW—BEING AND BECOMING

Short stories
THE JEWEL AND OTHER SHORT STORIES
Sci-Fi Series 1
Sci-Fi Series 2
Cats & Dogs Series

BEYOND RELIGION II

An Inquiry into the Nature of Being
A personal View

Stanisław Kapuściński
[aka Stan I.S. Law]

COLLECTED ESSAYS
VOLUME II

INHOUSEPRESS, MONTREAL, CANADA

Copyright © Stanislaw Kapuscinski 1999
http://stanlaw.ca
Ebook Edition 2011
Paperback 2015
All rights reserved. No part of this publication may be reproduced, stored in a retrieval system, or transmitted in any form or by any means electronic, mechanical, photocopying, recording or otherwise, without the prior written permission of the publisher.

Published by
INHOUSEPRESS
http://inhousepress.ca

Design and layout
Bozena Happach

ISBN 978-0-9731184-1-4

Paperback Edition 2015
INHOUSEPRESS

For my Mother

*"...what if we picked the wrong religion?
We'd make God madder and madder?*

Homer Simpson, (favorite comic strip character of Stephen Hawking),
explains why he no longer wants to visit a church on Sunday.

CONTENTS
List of Essays:

FOREWORD		11
INTRODUCTION		13
1. WITHIN & WITHOUT	Cracking the cosmic egg	17
2. BABOON	Dominion over our thoughts	21
3. SPACE, TIME & VIBRATIONS	On Einstein and the Spirit	25
4. BALANCE	The unreality of good and evil	29
5. BIRDS OF PARADISE	Love, attraction, oscillating universe	33
6. ORGANIZED MATTER	In search of Life	38
7. REINCARNATION	On Life, eternity, spiritual evolution	42
8. THE QUESTION OF SUICIDE	A question of ownership	46
9. REALITY	All is not as it seems	52
10. SPIRIT	The Ba Sotho of Transvaal	57
11. THE GOOD OL'DAYS	Devolution from Golden to Iron Age	61
12. WUNDERKIND	The loss of wholeness	67
13. ONE	I and my Father are One	71
14. NOW	The eternal present, evolution	75
15. MYSTERY	Nothing is hidden…	79
16. MIRACLES	Subjective and objective reality transfer	83
17. CRITICAL MASS	On leaven and changes to mass consciousness	87
18. THE ATHEIST	The teaching of Jesus	91
19. MORE ABOUT PRAYERS		95
20. RIGHTS	Our job on earth	99
21. THE ANTICHRIST		103
22. PAIN		107
23. ZEN AND THE BIBLE	A comparative glance	113
24. GROUPS	Archetypes of the "us and them" syndrome	117
25. TEMPTATION	Thoughts on the Lords Prayer	121
26. LIMITATIONS	Elimination of duality	125

List of essays, cont.:

#	Title	Description	Page
27.	HEAVEN	Different concepts	129
28.	DREAMING OR DOING NOTHING -	The woo wei	133
29.	PETER	More about faith	137
30.	THE GREATEST CRIME	Was Jesus God?	141
31.	WHAT IS CAESAR'S?	On literary interpretation of the Bible	145
32.	AQUARIUS & URANUS	Three lessons of the Zodiac	151
33.	I AM THAT I AM	The nature of God	157
34.	MARRIAGE	The attraction of the opposites	161
35.	FEAR	About reverence	165
36.	LOOPHOLES	On bypassing the laws of the universe	169
37.	COSMOS	A view of the universe	173
38.	SUBMISSION	Discussing the Koran	179
39.	TITHING	On giving, taking and sharing	185
40.	FUNDAMENTALISM	The broader picture	189
41.	AGING		193
42.	BABEL	On a book by Umberto Eco	199
43.	BLISS	On the concept of *dharma*	203
44.	SPIRITUAL LIFE	A Christian perspective	207
45.	THE FINAL VICTORY	Listening to my father	210
46.	POINTS OF VIEW		215
47.	A LITTLE BANG	On the origins of the universe	219
48.	VISIBILIUM OMNIUM OR 10% -	On the visible and invisible universe	225
49.	MIRROR	On perception of divinity	231
50.	THE DEVIL	On perception of reality	235
51.	THE UNDISCOVERED COUNTRY -	On the illusion of death	239
52.	BEYOND RELIGION II	A second essay on Spiritual Evolution	243

All essays carry the date of original writing. The dates are given as year, month and day. Thus *Baboon* had been written on 970616. Some additional notes and/or comments have been added in late autumn 1999 and 2010.

FOREWORD

It has been said that an evergreen song is one that you think you have heard before. You can't quite put your finger on as to where or when, but it sounds, or seems to sound, so familiar. So it is when one rediscovers Truth.

None of us have a monopoly on Truth. All we can do is try to remember when or where we heard this familiar tune before. And we all have heard it. It lingers latent in our individual, perhaps even racial memory. It touches us in our dreams, in our inexplicable desires, yens, sometimes in a feeling of unsatisfied hunger. When we remember a little better, we begin to feel a longing, homesickness, rather like Jack London's *The Call of the Wild.* Only our longing is not for the wonders of nature but rather for that which frees us from fetters, from irons of limitations which we all, at one time or another, have imposed on our wings. We want to fly, to taste the freedom, which only Truth can give us.

Whatever we read, hear, espy, we cannot accept, absorb, make it or own, unless the echo of that which we hear is already reverberating within us. We do not really learn from others. We do not really accept other's philosophy, nor other's religious convictions. We all tend to our gardens, to our own tiny universes, and we hope that, now and again, we shall see or hear from somewhere a word of encouragement. This slap on the back comes from finding, perhaps reading, a confirmation of what we have long suspected. Yet until we do read it, we feel lonely, uncertain. Then, finally, we come across someone who thinks in a similar vein, formulates or recognizes a vision of Truth, which heretofore has lain hidden from our timid eyes.

Yet the Truth can only come from within. The best I can hope for is to offer a verbal form, a semantic, linear expression of that which you have long suspected.

My efforts, essays, will be neither symphonies nor sonatas, but rather little airs, forgotten melodies, which I hope will strike a resonant note in your heart. I do not attempt to impress your intellect. Intellect calculates, the heart—feels. If you do recognize some melodies, don't be surprised. The Truth is One. And if any of my chords strike harmony within you, it only means that you and I found a way of looking at It from a similar vantage point. And what is more important, you will know that you are no longer alone.

***

INTRODUCTION

It has been said that there is nothing new in the world. There are those who claim that the manifested universe had already been created in the form of innumerable states of consciousness, and all we must do is to enter them in order to gather experience.

But this is like saying that all I have to do is to go to the Louvre in order to see the Mona Lisa. It's true, of course, but in order to do so I must have the means of travel. I must know how to get there and when I do, how to recognize the painting. There are many fake "Mona Lisas". In other words, I need knowledge. And here we come to the crux of the matter. We must know what, where and how. It is this trio, which, perhaps in a manner not immediately apparent, I am exploring in this group of essays. While the methods of travel are relatively few, the personal preferences of the travelers are as diverse as the population of this planet. Furthermore, some Ways are more suitable than others for travelers in various stages of their journeys. Heretofore, the methods have been identified by various religions. Alas, the era of orthodox religions is coming to an end. In ever increasing numbers, people will embark on individual journeys, as individual as their fingerprints, the patterns of their irises, or their genetic code.

In these essays I endeavor to explore the various options. Some readers will, I hope, forgive me that I tend to rely mostly, though not exclusively, on the tenets proposed in the Bible. This is due to the conditioning of my early years, though the signposts I discovered later in the same biblical sources are at great divergence from those initially imposed on me by my teachers. My present premise is that only a mental movement from the known towards the unknown can achieve progress. I dare to reach beyond the known.

BEYOND... RELIGION.

The Truth, as I see It, has been declared many times by various avatars. Later, their teachings appear to have been adapted to the needs of the few, to enable them to wield power over the many. I believe it is time to free ourselves from all constrains. In order to bring the point home, I shall endeavor to present the same Truth from many different angles. It may occasionally seem repetitious, but then... the "counter truth", the "great Sham" has been repeated more often than I could possibly do in these pages. To protect yourself from possible tedium, I suggest not reading my essays more often than one or two per week. If you allow the new, yet so very, very old concepts to permeate your mindset, the succeeding essays will gradually strike you as only vaguely familiar. Truth has the quality of being absorbed by osmosis. Once absorbed, it becomes your own.

I try to show an alternate view to the generally accepted orthodox tenets. It is not my intention to convince anyone of my own sentiments, but rather to share with you a different point of view than that presented by most people dealing with such subjects. Often, I shall sketch different scenarios, as in the *Question of Suicide*, in order to compel the reader to form his or her own opinion. If fact, this is true of most of my essays. By all means, prove me wrong. I've been wrong many times before. I find that I learn most by my mistakes.

There is but one axiom I do state with utmost conviction: No matter how many books we read, how many ancient manuscripts we study, no matter how many buttons we twist... the only truth which will set us free is the Truth which we shall find, ultimately, within ourselves. And then, for the rest of our lives we shall struggle to rediscover It again and again. Perhaps it gets easier with time. And if the pages that follow will whet your appetite, if my thoughts will goad you to set out on your own search, on your own conscious journey, then I will not have written in vain.

We have long entered the Age of Aquarius. The essay on the subject discusses the many implications of this fascinating Zodiacal age. The important thing to remember is that, as of now, according to the Zodiac, we must all cultivate our own, individual gardens. The method of pass-the-buckmanship is over. Your garden awaits you and the richness of the fruit it shall bear depends only on you.

Happy gardening.

***

1
WITHIN AND WITHOUT

What is Reality? Mystics assure us that God is all in all. ALL IN ALL. Is God the quintessence of Reality? Most religions affirm that God is One. And having said it, they spent their waken hours promulgating the duality of every aspect of Reality. They preach about God *and* the Devil; about good *and* evil; the holy *and* the profane; heaven *and* hell; the saintly *and* the satanic; spirit *and* matter; yin *and* yang;(1) YAHWEH;(2) the sheep *and* the goats; rewards *and* punishments; rights *and* wrongs. At least, yin and yang are said to represent two sides of the same coin. No one says this of God and Devil. Symbolically or not, all religions base their creeds on duality. Whatever happened to the omnipresent Oneness?

And if we are to search for Truth, are we to look within or without?

For a season, we had been preoccupied with little more than sustaining our biological existence. Physical survival was the name of the game. It was the only game in town. Hand-to-mouth, dog-eat-dog, type of existence. Left to ourselves, we tended to regard the world from our puny, internalized point or view. We limited our horizons to our own experience, to the knowledge imprinted on our genes, our subconscious: our animal souls. We created our own realities, our own tiny universes. We proudly gazed at the inner surfaces of our personal, tiny cosmic eggs.

Enter religions.

Suddenly, there was a universe outside our carefully constructed havens. The religions challenged our introverted realities. Arts, temples, ideas sprang to life, all vastly exceeding the shelf-life of our individual survival. Religions shattered our internalized sense of security.(3) They provided the necessary impetus to wean us from our egocentric wombs. They strove to crack, often brutally, our carefully constructed cosmic eggs. They assailed our protective layers, the armor we developed over aeons of evolution. We stepped outside. Gradually our eyes become adjusted to a new light, to the wonder of an ever expanding, ever receding horizon. The family, the clan, the nation, then the earth, the solar system, the galaxy, then billions upon billions of galaxies filled our vision.

If God is all in all, then God expanded exponentially.

Today, while many political and religious leaders continue to build empires, the world is well on its way to becoming a global village. While religions continue to offer reward after death, the faithful are busy discovering heaven here and now. Centuries of exploitation metamorphosed into continuous exploration. People are learning to live in the present, not to procrastinate the gift of life for a distant, uncertain tomorrow. Within a reality in which we can circumnavigate the world in a few hours, time loses its meaning.

Enter Age of Aquarius!

A strange statistic was published recently. It reported that while fewer people attend religious services, increasing numbers search for spiritual truth. A paradox? Not really. The religions have done their job. They opened our eyes, cracked our cosmic eggs. They introduced us to many gods. Gods of power, illusion, small-jealous-vindictive gods. But also to gods of music, of poetry, of beauty. Finally to the God of Love. We have outgrown all but the last few of them. Apparently, we have also outgrown religions. Next to the grandeur of the Universe, Olympus has shrunk to an anthill.

Science continues to push the fringes of infinity beyond our understanding. For countless generations we gazed at the stars, searching for gods. We looked *Without*, while the universe continued to expand. We could no longer find gods within the infinity of space. Yet our hunger remained. The final dichotomy.

And then, finally, we turned to look *Within*.

We had come a full circle. Once we stood within and looked outward with a sadly myopic vision. Now, we stand outside and look within. Perhaps the kingdom of God really is within us.(4) But how? How can the Infinite be contained within the finite? To our astonishment we discover that the Within is equally endless, that It manifests the very same infinity which the Without offered. We can no longer give up. We remember that nothing will remain hidden.(5) In 1945 an Arab peasant stumbled across an earthenware container. Fourteen years later, the first authoritative translation of, what became known as, the Gospel of Thomas was published, one of 52 tractates of the Nag Hammadi Library. In it lies our answer: *Kingdom is within you and it is without you.*(6)

Could it be that duality is but an illusion?

Within *and* Without. Kingdom is all there is. There is nothing but the Kingdom. There is no duality. Heaven is One. Heaven is *Reality*. It is a state of consciousness. Nature, all nature, every tiny fragment of it, is an indivisible part of a single Reality. Thomas Moore wrote that nature is the prime source of spiritual life.(7) Whatever was, or will be, or could be—forms an integral part of that which Is. Beyond time, beyond space, within time, within space. There are no limits. We, standing outside our cosmic eggs, perceive Reality in a distant supernova, in the gossamer tail of a transient comet, in the hills and valleys of earth, in the paintings of the great masters, in Mozart's symphonies, in Bach's cantatas. We sense it in the trusting gaze of our lover. It is manifest in the innocence of a newborn baby, the furrowed brow of a concerned father. It is heard in the whisper of the wind, in the roar of the ocean. It is manifest in a tiniest bug crawling along a footpath; stepping on it we step on the life-force manifest in its movements. The very same life-force that enlivens our own bodies.

The Within and the Without are inseparable. They are the cause and the effect.

Cause and Effect—joined by the intransigence of the creative process. The Creation cannot be apart from Its Creator. Self-generating, ever indivisible, ever One. Immortal. Infinite. Omnipresent One. There is no duality.

WE ARE ONE.

***

970709

FOOTNOTES

1. Passive-female and the active-male principle of the universe. (Chinese philosophy).
2. *Yod, Hé, Wau, Hé* (the Hebrew tetragrammaton YAHWEH) represents the universal masculine and feminine principles (later anglicized to Jehovah).
3. compare: "...from henceforth there shall be five in one house divided, three against two and two against three. The father shall be divided against the son, and the son against the father, the mother against the daughter..." etc. Luke 12:52-53. The house, of course, symbolizes our state of consciousness; various members of your family symbolize different mindsets or concepts. The odd number (five) suggest the unlikelihood of balance.
4. Luke 17:21
5. For nothing is secret that shall not be made manifest: neither any thing hid, that shall not be known and come abroad" Luke 8:17, also Matthew 10:26
6. Koester, Helmut and Lambdin, Thomas O., (translators) THE GOSPEL ACCORDING TO THOMAS. [Harper & Raw 1990 © E.J.Brill]. (Logion 3) Also refer to Kapuscinski, Stanislaw THE KEY TO IMMORTALITY, [Inhousepress, Montreal 2001]
7. Moore, Thomas THE RE-ENCHANTMENT OF EVERYDAY LIFE [Harper Perennial, A Div. of Harper Collins Publishers].

2
BABOON

Baboon is a large ape. He has an elongated muzzle like that of a dog, strong tusks, a short tail, cheek-pouches, small, deep-set eyes with huge eyebrows and naked callosities on the buttocks. He shares his cognomen with an ugly or uncouth person although he is neither ugly nor uncouth, and has absolutely no desire to dominate man. Man, on the other hand, wishes to dominate the baboon. Some say, man was *created* to dominate the baboon—indeed, the world.

***

Sad to say, there is as much harm perpetrated by the orthodox religious propaganda as there is good resulting from the faithful who think for themselves. I am not suggesting that there are no priests or monks, or other members to the sacerdotal fraternity representing the multifarious religions, who are blind to the Truth. What I am saying is that the moment such members attempt to act as channels for the Truth, they are instantly stifled by their superiors, their elders, for whom the *status quo* guaranties power, control, dominion. The great scriptures of the world endeavor to lift humanity above the fog of insidious, if illusory, materiality imposed by the various religions. The churches, in their turn, twist, inveigle and distort the epiphanic revelations to meet their ends. To perpetrate their dominion over the faithful.

To perpetrate their dominion... Surely, dominion means control, and control abrogates freedom. And freedom is a fundamental gift of God.
Today the faithful, tomorrow the world!
What dictator, what church leader, does not aspire to such *dictum*? Dominion! Power! All in the name of the divine revelation—of course.

In the West, where the Judeo-Christian traditions predominate, there are people who hold that dominion over nature is their divine right. Equally, they claim their right to exploit the world, to torture innocent animals in tax-deductible laboratories, in order to prolong the biological functions of the stagnating bodies of the rich-and-famous. Such people often assert this divine right by citing the book of Genesis:

> *"And God said, Let us make man in our image, after our likeness: and let them have dominion over the fish of the sea, and over the fowl of the air, and over the cattle, and over all the earth, and over every creeping thing that creepeth upon the earth."* (1:26).

This single sentence has been wantonly misinterpreted in order to give license to kill, mutilate, torture, waste, pervert, debase, pollute, vanquish, manipulate, distort and generally abuse our place in the universe. As long as man will continue to regard the Bible as a textbook of anything but *spiritual* knowledge, the western religions will continue to ruin our habitat. [I say western because Buddhism is absolved of this perversion]. Any attempt to interpret the Bible as dealing with anything but soul, be it animal (Hebrew *nephesh*) or the divine spark (*El*), will invariably lead to the creation of religions which will build altars to their own glory at the expense of nature.

We all share in this ignominy, but none more than those in authority.

We must exercise great caution towards all who arrogate jurisdiction in all subjects dealing with the interpretation of the Bible. Particularly towards those who claim infallibility in these matters. No wonder the Christ despised the sacerdotal class. Whoever doubts my sentiments let him read Matthew 23:13 and the next few verses.

In case any doubt remains in anyone's mind, my own stance in this matter is that we, the people, hold no dominion over others. Human or animal.
Dominions are earned, not given.

What the contentious paragraph from Genesis teaches is that we are to learn control over our lower nature. The fish, the fowl of the air, the cattle, the whole earth, even every creeping thing: "that creepeth upon the earth", all symbolize *our thoughts*. The deep thoughts of the sea; the ephemeral thoughts, as light as the fowl of the air; the common, stable thoughts of our everyday life; the tiny, insignificant thoughts, the supposedly unimportant ones... they all churn within our consciousness and tend to become manifest in the material world. The "earth" symbolizes our physical consciousness. It is the sum-total of all our thoughts. Later the Bible refers to thoughts as sheep, and to the man who'd learned control over them, as good shepherd. All thoughts are building blocks in the world we call our reality. We create our universes with them—only to blame others for our fate. This is our dominion. The realm of our consciousness. This, and nothing else.

***

So if anyone had abused his or her body, and destroyed his or her internal organs, don't let them tear out the heart of a baboon, who lived his life according to the laws of nature. Let us not kill the innocent in order to protect the guilty. And if some were to be so misguided as to do so, at least don't let them do it the name of God. Or the scriptures.

We must learn control over our thoughts. The material universe would not exist without them. Who knows... perhaps, one day, we shall all learn to live in harmony with nature. Like the rest of the animal kingdom.

And let us not call men baboons any more. The baboon is a beautiful and noble creature. And man is much too uncouth.

***

970616

FOOTNOTES

1. In 1984, "Baby Fae's" baboon-heart transplant sparked public debate... In 1964, doctors first placed a chimpanzee's heart into a human being.

When they hear of the Way,
The highest minds practice it;
The average minds think about it
And try it now and then;
The lowest minds laugh at it.
It they did not laugh at it,
It would not be the Way.

Lao Tse

3
SPACE, TIME & VIBRATIONS

I know of no literate man who hasn't heard about the equation $E=MC^2$. Considerably fewer people can visualize what it means. Fewer still are fully cognizant of its consequences. Yet Albert Einstein, thought by many to have been a revolutionary physicist, was, and to me will always remain, a great mystic. As great a mystic as any depicted in the Bible. Primarily, for two reasons.

Einstein stated that if we accelerate any object to the velocity of light the mass of the object would become infinite. Simultaneously, the very same dilation would apply to time; every second would stretch longer and longer until it would last forever. Should we travel aboard a spaceship capable of such velocities, we would become both: omnipresent and immortal—at least in the eyes of those remaining on earth, tracing our progress towards infinity. Strangely enough, the astronauts themselves (that's us—we are all hurling through space on our spaceship 'soul'), would experience neither the swelling of our bodies, nor a sense of slowing of time. We, within our own, albeit unique, environment, would continue as if nothing has happened.

A paradox? Perhaps, yet the Bible has foretold such a turn of events a few thousand years ago—in its own enigmatic, symbolic way. It said: *According to your faith be it unto you.*(1) Subjective reality remains subjective. Einstein just took is a step further.

The Bible asserts that certain circumstances quicken our spirit. In the Bible, to "quicken" means to give or to preserve life(2). Now if spirit can be quickened(3), it can also be "slowed down". And this is precisely what happened to us. We humans, flora and fauna, the physical world, are all made up of spirit slowed down. We, as spiritual entities, are states of consciousness accumulating spiritual attributes. The more and the purer our universal attributes, *the higher (more quickened) our vibrations*, the greater, the more luminous our body. Taking Einstein's concept one step further, to become omnipresent and immortal we do no have to travel from A to B at high velocities. We must quicken our spirit, our awareness of life, of who and what we really are. Until we do that, we shall continue to move around at a snail's pace, identifying with our physical, material bodies, as our only heritage. We seem to have forgotten our natural state of being, shed our natural attributes; in a sense, we became... no longer alive. At least this is what the Bible calls all who had forgotten their true nature.(4)

The biblical term "quickening" also refers to vibrations. All matter vibrates. Mystics, saints, some poets, great artists, all advanced beings, can sense these oscillations; they perceive them as sound. Some call it the Music of the Spheres. This heavenly music is omnipresent, eternal. Others refer to it as the Life force, the Chi, still others call it the Holy Spirit.(5) No matter what the name, none can be accurate, all can but approximate the Essence of Life. They all refer to a "substance" from which we are made, which also sustains us, which is unlimited in Its potential.

Yet most of us cannot hear these vibrations. Many deny their existence. They might as well deny the existence of radio waves, of television transmissions, or X-rays. After all, they all vibrate. Some will say "aah, but these are forms of energy." To which Einstein replies "aah, but matter and energy are interchangeable. That's exactly what $e=mc^2$ is all about!"

Thank you Albert, I couldn't have put it better myself!(6)

So where do we go from here? How do you explain the beauty of Beethoven's symphony to one born deaf?

Back to the Bible and the quickening of the spirit. Now that we know that we are spiritual beings whose vibrations have been substantially slowed down, all we must do is to find out how to accelerate our vibratory rate. As we do, we shall gradually ascend the scale of spirituality, until we become omnipresent and immortal. How? There are some aspects of our being which retain these high vibrations. These are love, appreciation of beauty, compassion, a sense of oneness, and many others. These traits, as real as our material traits, are the attributes of our Essence which is already outside the constrains of time and space. If we love someone, his or her presence thousands of miles away from us does in no way diminish our love. Equally, we even continue to love those who left their physical envelopes. These few traits, which are unbound by time or space, are Aspects of Soul. Soul is both omnipresent and immortal; like love, It is indestructible. The same cannot be said about the temporary prisons that we have created. These prisons slow down our vibrations but they accelerate the rate of learning. That is the purpose of duality, which is a quality of *lower vibrations only*. Yet freedom, true freedom, is another aspect of Soul. It has little to do with the removal of physical constrains. Some manage to remain free within the confines of iron bars. Their bodies are shackled; their souls remain free. Others are prisoners of their own weaknesses. A drug addict, a smoker, an alcoholic, anyone believing in their limitations, are all slaves, handcuffed by their own erroneous thinking. Some will not believe in any of this. Those who do, took, or will shortly take, their first tentative steps towards immortality.

By the way, Einstein also said that one cannot achieve the velocity of light and remain "solid matter". It stands to reason. To move an infinite mass would require infinite energy. The two would cancel each other out. Once we quicken our spirit, once we convert all our atoms into energy: we are no longer solid matter. We are no longer subject to the laws governing coarse material objects. We become Beings of Light. We'll no longer have to say: "Beam me us, Scotty!" We would already be there. For as long as we wish. Even forever.

***
970713

FOOTNOTES

1. Matthew 9:29
2. Hebrew *chayah* Psalms 71:20, 80:18, 119:25, et al; Greek *zoopoieo* John 5:21, 6:63, also in Romans, 1 Corinthians, 1 Timothy, et al.
3. "It is the spirit that quickeneth; the flesh profiteth nothing" John 6:63. This means that the flesh is always the result, not the cause.
4. We find an example of this thesis in Christ's words: Let the dead bury their dead. (Matthew 8:22)
5. The same energy is identified by others as Qi (Chi), Vis Vitalis, Prana, Divine Power, etc.. Since it is a non-physical force any attempt to identify it exactly is futile. We can only observe It by the trails It leaves behind. Rather like quarks in a cyclotron.
6. $E=MC^2$ stands for: Energy = Mass x the Velocity of Light squared. Light is reckoned to travel at 186,000 miles, or 300,000 km. per second, in a void. The equation suggests what incredible potential energy we carry in our physical bodies! It is suggestive of the power of Spirit.

The universe resounds with the joyful cry, I AM.

Aleksandre Nikolayevich Scriabin
(1872-1915)

4
BALANCE

To repeat yet again, in absolute terms, All is One. Not the world, the innumerable galaxies, but the State of Consciousness. The stars are but the expressions of the countless states into which the One seems able to individualize Itself. The same is true of every material object or entity, of incident or attribute. The individualizations that are endowed with self-awareness, we call souls. In fact, there is only one Soul. Like all divine attributes, It is One yet capable of countless individual expressions. The word "individual" comes to us from Latin: *individualis* or *individuus*, meaning indivisible, inseparable. And this single Consciousness seems bent on sharing Its divine attributes with Its own creation, with all that are capable, or willing, to do so. It created milliards of hypothetical states into which we, the nascent units of awareness can enter, learn and advance. But we are not independent. We are as reliant on the One as a babe-in-arms is reliant upon the unconditional love of its mother. Without it, the babe dies. With it—it prospers. In time, hardly understanding the process, the babe grows up and asserts its own individuality. Sadly, it often forgets whence it came...

For the purpose of bringing the nascent individuality back to its source, the One makes a concession. Divine Wisdom, i.e. the elusive state of balance between infinite intelligence and infinite love, splits. We recognize this attribute of Divine Wisdom as duality. Like all conditions of dilution, duality is a state as transient as all that is imperfect. Only the state of balance is permanent.
Only the state Itself, not Its components.

All that we refer to as "good" or "evil" is unreal. Such states of consciousness lack reality because they, like all that is diluted, are relative. The very same thought, action or event can serve as a whole spectrum of moral discrimination. Generous thoughts translated into charitable donations for children in Ethiopia extended the war between warring factions by many years. The donations haven't reached the children—they fed the rebels fighting for control, for power. A speeding ambulance can save someone's life, kill a stray dog, child, an elderly person reacting too slowly to its mission mercy. A knife in the hands of a discontented neurotic kills; in the hands of a surgeon prolongs lives. Same thoughts, same actions, same objects—different effects. None are good, none evil. There is nothing intrinsically good about prolonging a stagnating life, nothing intrinsically bad about assisting in its termination. Yet nothing is useless if it serves to teach us something.

Teach whom? Who is "us"?

We are all individualized states of consciousness. Though matter is transient—the consciousness goes on. Biological matter soon disintegrates, emotions last longer, ideas hold sway over generations. Consciousness lasts forever. We can kill a man's body; we cannot kill his soul. He cannot even destroy it himself. What he can do, however, is to lose track of it. All is subject to what we believe in, i.e. what we have encoded in our subconscious. If we don't believe in immortality, we are not immortal. The soul, however, for whom we provided a temporary home—is. We *do not have a soul*, though, for a short while, the Soul tries hard to have us. One at a time. Aren't we lucky?

The soul within us is that which is in a state of balance. When we accept this condition of being, we become one with the soul.

A State of Balance.

BALANCE

Buddha called it the Middle Path. Not the good or the bad, the saintly or the profane. The *Middle* Path. The path that is non-judgmental: every judgement requires a mental descent into dualistic reality. The Middle Path recognizes that all is One. No matter how we fragment our way of thinking, our perceptions will ultimately flow together again. Echoing the Middle Path, the Yin and the Yang are neither good nor bad; they are the general terms for the opposite forces which work at all times to remain in balance.(1) In Tao Te Ching, the Chinese Master Lao-Tzu admonishes us to give up all striving. This state of consciousness, devoid of strife, of anger or envy, where no wars or struggles upset the divine state of balance, the Bible calls Jerusalem. The city of Peace. The state of mind beyond human understanding. Rumi, the great Sufi poet said: *"It is necessary to note, that opposite things work together, even though nominally opposed.*(2)

In a dualistic world we must strive to maintain balance.

It seems futile to discuss, let alone insist, which is better: the gravitational pull of the sun or the centrifugal force inherent in the movement of the planets. Is one good—the other evil? What nonsense! Too much of one, and we plunge into the nuclear inferno. Too much of the other, and we destroy all biological and zoological life by freezing them in the black void of space. Both forces are equally destructive if one takes pre-eminence over the other.

Within the realm of our immaturity, *for every opinion we hold an equal and opposite opinion will manifest itself.* Somewhere—through someone.

Every extreme philosophy, every extreme political system, every intolerant religion, every deadly weapon will find its opposite. Some think it noble to resist evil.(3) Yet it is futile and unnecessary. By resistance we only uphold the illusion of its reality. Isn't it wiser to turn the other cheek? The balance will be restored, regardless of our intercession. Many people regard the Law of Karma as a Damoclesian sword of justice hanging over their heads. Some grow so afraid of its illusory menace that they try to resist its dictates. Yet the sole purpose of the Law of Karma is to restore balance—a condition upset by our ignorance. In a way, the Law of Karma is the law of inexhaustible mercy. It extends its credit for untold millions of years. It can be thought of as the divine attribute of patience.

All opposites are but an illusion. The Truth is always in the middle. Within the middle path. After all, isn't God that which the opposites have in common?

***

970719

FOOTNOTES

1. Originally, yin and yang probably referred to the 'sunless' and 'sunny', (as in sides of the mountain). Then they came to mean 'female' and 'male'. Only later the terms grew to represent the principles of dualistic nature.
2. Fihi Ma Fihi. Jalal-ud-Din Rumi 1207 - 1273. (also known as Jalaluddin Rumi)
3. Compare Matthew 5:39.

*Even though you tie a hundred knots
the string remains one.*

Jalal-ud-Din Rumi

5
BIRDS OF PARADISE

Any man lucky enough to witness the elaborate courtship of the Birds of Paradise will be put to shame. The male of the species works hard to attract the female. An affair as long and elaborate as it is beautiful; an expression of such desire, such adoration, dare I say... love, that man's paltry expressions of like sentiments towards his intended, pale by comparison. There are many other members of the animal, bird, and even insect kingdoms, which inspired me to demonstrate greater attraction for my better half, indicative of more attention, more care and affection than I thought, heretofore, necessary or expedient. Yet, compared to the Birds of Paradise, I lag far behind. Surely, an expression of attraction is a direct demonstration of love. Could it be that nature, or that which we call life, is sustained by the most fundamental energy of the universe? No, not the inherent instinct for self-preservation, but love. Love and life seem synonymous. And can there be love without attraction?

Attraction is love in action. The dynamics of attraction is love.

In human terms, we demonstrate love at four levels.

First, there is purely physical attraction which, at one time or another, is enjoyed by most people. Sexual fulfillment is its reward, though few participants realize that their moment of delight is but a shadow of higher forms of love.

At the second level we succumb to emotional attraction. Most people tend to confuse love with emotion, with a "feeling" we have for one another or for non-reciprocative objects such as music, knowledge, fame or even money. Regardless of perfunctory denials, there is ample evidence that many people have compromised their "love" for a person for more abstract pursuits. The emotional attraction is, directly or indirectly, responsible for excesses in tribalism, nationalism, and fundamentalism of every sort. This type of love often results in uncontrollable passion, devoid of rationality, responsibility or even compassion.

The third manifestation of love is fuelled by our intellect. This form of attraction, though seemingly devoid of passion or irrational entanglements, is as powerful as the previous expression, often to the exclusion of other considerations. Einstein sacrificed his marriage, family, religion and national affiliation to pursue his all-consuming attraction for the mysteries of the universe. He was more faithful to his chosen attraction than many a swain to his lady.

Finally we come to the highest form of love, the force which attracts us, inexorably, to the highest, the best, the supreme. This form of attraction results in unconditional love, a state of consciousness that fills us with a sublime, if often subliminal, awareness of being one with All. In this form of expression, the object of our attraction and we become one. Some call this a manifestation of Divine Love.

Didn't you ever wonder why the many mystics so often stressed the importance of love? Whichever form of expression we choose to demonstrate, love is always manifested as attraction, as that which joins and keeps us together, regardless of any and all the forces which endeavor to pull us apart. Be it the Divine, unconditional love, or the divine feeling of being in love, both are inherently expressed by attraction. It cannot be otherwise. And if it is so, if love is fundamental to the functioning of the universe, how does it manifest itself? How does this attraction work?

Without it, not a single species inhabiting our earth would survive. All that assures the preservation of any species is the law of attraction. Love, if you prefer. Let us go further. If it weren't for attraction, the electrons would leave their nuclei and fly off, probably smash into other nuclei. A chain reaction on universal scale would follow. Thank heaven for attraction! Then we have the atoms themselves with all their appurtenances: the neutrons, protons, all the way down to the quarks. What keeps them together? What stops you, and me, from literally disintegrating into a mass of swirling subatomic particles? The physicists call them gluons, particles that bind quarks together with *strong* force. No wonder they call it strong. The strongest there is! A *strong*, binding attraction. Love? Perhaps. Perhaps some atoms just... love being together.

At any rate, I am glad they are attracted to each other.

There is also chemical attraction or affinity, which unites molecules of a different kind; cohesive attraction uniting adjacent molecules of the same nature; there are magnetic, diamagnetic and electrical attractions... I think the universe is in love!

Next we have the sun and the planets—our earth among them. Here the scientists would probably sound a bit silly if they said that the sun is in love with the planets. Yet there is no doubt that if the sun did not attract its planets, we would be frozen to death, within minutes, in the abyss of deep space. The earth is ever pulling away from the sun—the centrifugal force is powerful, but love is stronger. The sun aims to keep us wrapped in warmth, for as long as we need it. Did you ever wonder why?

And now we come to the greatest expression of this indispensable law.

Children are taught in school about the Big Bang: the explosion that, billions of years ago (some scientists tell us), gave birth to our universe. It also initiated the outward motion of all matter—the progenitor of the centrifugal force.

Will this outward movement continue forever? Shall we drift, with all the billions of galaxies, further and further away from each other, until our own galaxy—later our solar system—is left forlorn in the vastness of frozen space? Could it be that there is a force in the universe stronger than the force of attraction?

For many years the scientists have been worried. They could not find sufficient matter in the universe which would add up to enough mass to slow down the outward journey of the galaxies and, eventually, to initiate the homeward voyage. To initiate the centripetal movement. Then, over the years, our physicists discovered the "black matter". Later, they suspected that the black holes could be tiny, obviously invisible, and litter the universe in vast numbers. Such black holes would add enormous, if immeasurable, quantities of matter to the totality of mass in the universe. Finally, recently, the scientists began to suspect that every galaxy must have a gargantuan black hole at its center, which would offer sufficient gravitational pull to maintain all the billions of stars within the system from escaping its influence. Talk of love! Sorry, ah... attraction...

Well before any of our illustrious scientists thought about it, the sages of the murky past knew that there is sufficient matter to cause the universe to collapse upon itself. They called it the Oscillating Universe. Or the day and the night of Brahma.(1) Or the breathing out and the breathing in of God. No matter—they knew. The cosmologists now call it the Big Bang—Big Crunch theory. Whatever happens, the law of attraction will rule supreme.

Or... the law of Love.

All our scientists had to do was to look at the Birds of Paradise. The seemingly absurd conclusion, the consummation of the dance of love, can be measured in seconds—one or two, at most. In fact, the consummation of the dance of love is so short that it seems almost incidental to the ritual. Like the final collapse into a Black Hole, where both time and space cease to be. What seems to matter to the

Birds of Paradise is the expression of attraction, of desire, of... again love seems to come to mind, rather than its fulfillment. Perhaps the act of preservation of the species is only a by-product of the inherent need to express one's love. If not for us, humans, then at least for the Birds of Paradise. Sex is a utilitarian, if enjoyable, function, practiced by the most primitive forms of life. But only the Birds of Paradise have relegated it to an afterthought; a fragmentary addition to a wondrous, incredibly beautiful ritual of attraction. What the male bird offers its mate, and vicariously to us all, is nothing less than the expression of the highest law of the universe.

We all live in Paradise, basking in the realm of Infinite Love. Who knows? Perhaps, one day, we shall learn to emulate the birds.

***

970728

FOOTNOTES

1. It is my opinion that the ancient sages had been referring not to the Universe but to our galaxy, which to all intent and purpose is our universe. It seems more logical to assume that the Milky Way will, one day, collapse into its own Black Hole, than to assign the same fate to the rest of the Universe, about which we still know very little.

6
ORGANIZED MATTER

Life is a state of functional activity and continual change peculiar to organized matter...
states the Concise Oxford Dictionary.

Webster offers a slightly different opinion:
that *property of plants and animals*
(that's us, by the way, at least most people I know)
which makes it possible for them to take in food, get energy from it, grow, adapt themselves to their surroundings, and reproduce their kind.

I often lack energy—particularly when overfed; being a loner—I'm rather badly adapted to my surroundings and, alas, I have no progeny. I'm probably dead, at least according to Mr. Noah Webster L.L.D.. I would respectfully suggest that if there are other animals such as I, something must be missing from both definitions. Unless many of us are zombies... The living dead? Surely, there must be more to *life* than "organized matter capable of feeding and reproducing itself?"

The Oxonian scholars have established that life manifests itself as a continual change. But what of the *in*animate matter? Look at the tides, look at the explosive corona of our sun. Look at the myriad atoms swirling in a single speck of dust! It would seem that life, whatever it might be, is a peculiarity of only *some* matter, since the atoms are also intricately organized, and certainly involved in a functional activity—all around us.

If life is change, then life is omnipresent.

And then we meet a man who said, *"I am... the life."*(1) Somehow I doubt that Jesus of Nazareth, to whom this unorthodox statement is attributed, had "organized-self-reproducing-matter" in mind. I doubt that he had any matter in mind. Organized or otherwise.

So, once again, what is life?

We know that there is a time, a brief fragment of eternity, in which whatever we define as life leaves our bodies. There was a time when we defined our bodies themselves as life, yet, in that terminal moment of truth, it seems otherwise. It seems that we are not life, rather that life is within us. So what did the author of the above statement mean when he said, "I am the life"? What was he that we are not? Are we life also? Are you life? Who is this you, or I, for that matter? Is the life within you and me, different?

And there's the rub. We don't seem to take much trouble to find out what, let alone who, we are. We describe ourselves as functions: as jobs, occupations or professions we perform. I'm a doctor, says a fat unhealthy man. I am an architect, affirms a man who never erected a structure of beauty. I am a father, a mother. How quaint! So is every male and female of the animal kingdom. All animals absorb food, gather energy from it, and procreate. In what way are we different from them?

Are we different?

I am the resurrection and the life.(2)

Resurrection? Don't we have to die before we get resurrected? Apparently not. Conversely, there are other definitions of life than those offered by the scholars.

Whosoever liveth and believeth in me shall never die.(3)

Come on! Everyone dies. It is the law of nature. All organized matter dies. We stop eating, procreating, and we die. Never die? Really!

...he that beliveth in me, though he were dead, yet shall he live.

Now, either someone is trying to confuse us, or Messrs. Webster and Fowler(4) have never read the Bible. Rather strange considering that the Scriptures are clearly defined and extensively quoted in both dictionaries. I do not suggest for a moment that either of the gentlemen should profess to any Christian or Judaic creed. I am suggesting that their definition of life might be slightly different had either of them actually read the compendium of books known as the Bible, which I find an incredible source of knowledge not found anywhere else. None of the information therein has anything whatever to do with any religion. Just with everyday living.

In fact—with life!

Life, it appears, has none of the characteristics defined by our illustrious scholars. In fact, it is none of the above. Although it does find its expression in, or through, continual change, itself it remains changeless. Rather like an ocean continually pounding the shore, evaporating and replenishing its waters, yet seemingly remaining constant. It is certainly not a function of ingesting food or procreation. Life is. IS. It is in the same category as Love. As Spirit. As Soul. It is an attribute of the Infinite which, on occasion, chooses to individualize Itself in a biological form. At one level of intensity It is present in everything. At another level, Life is a state of... not change, as the Oxonians would have us believe, but a state of Consciousness. It is permanent, omnipresent, and indestructible. Only Its vehicles change.

As I mentioned before, Life IS.

We can spend millennia trying to define It. We can't. Like all the divine traits, It is beyond mental comprehension. It manifests Itself in infinite diversity. The best we can do is observe It, enjoy Its presence, for the duration It chooses to use us as Its channels. There is a way to experience It, but trying to understand It with our minds is futile. We can't use mind to know mind. Freud made that mistake. So did countless scientists. They all settled for second best. They all studied the effects, never the Cause. Rather like our physicians. They give us pills to alleviate pain. The cause of pain remains. Like our ignorance.

It seems that for all of us who identify our state of consciousness with organized matter, the late Joseph Campbell was right when he said: *"Life has no meaning. What is the meaning of a rose?"*

***

970813

FOOTNOTES

1. John 14:6
2. ibid. 11:25
3. ibid
4. H.W. Fowler and F.G. Fowler are the first editors of the Concise Oxford Dictionary.

> *Life is only the memory of a dream.*
> *It comes from no visible rain.*
> *It falls into no recognizable sea.*
>
> Sai Baba

7
REINCARNATION

The concept dealing with the continuity of life is based on the assumption that we, in one form or another, are immortal. Admittedly, it is a rather portentous assumption, but... could *all* the avatars, saviors, saints, mystics, ancient philosophers and even the resulting religions be wrong? All of them? When discussing reincarnation we are not discussing birth or death; we are discussing life stretching into eternity. And that's a very, very long time! Given a choice of spending perpetuity reclining on a celestial puffy cloud of happiness while listening, for the umpteenth time, to the sweet strains of an angelic harp... versus re-entering a new body endowed with new talents and possibilities, facing new challenges, crossing new horizons, rejoicing in new perspectives of the universe, well... to each his own. I know which I would pick.

And I did.

There is a peculiar consequence of one's choice. Since, even a cursory observation of life will confirm that whatever we truly believe in is, or becomes, our reality, the choice we make is of paramount importance. Oh, if we choose the "puffy cloud" due to our aversion to challenges etc., we will still, eventually, be re-incarnated. But we shall probably end up in circumstances that we had chosen. We shall inhabit a dull body with a dull, puffy, brain. After all, we did want to do nothing for eternity, right?

Reality is like that. According to our innermost desire, some call it faith (1), our fate is written. Providing we don't contradict the universal laws: like not wanting to get reincarnated at all, or wanting to be a vegetable. If we hope for the latter, we probably will be, but in a human form. Get the drift? Our innermost beliefs shape our destiny. No one controls our puppet strings. We and we alone control our destiny. We are the victims and the executioners. We are gods! (2)

Back to the concept of life.
Life is static. As established (hopefully) in the previous essay: Life is. Life is that which permeates the universe as the basic force, energy, if you like. As already mentioned, some people call it Spirit. And it is because Life (3), though static, refuses to lull in the heavenly doldrums eternally twiddling Its potential creativity, that It needs vehicles to become dynamic. Matter, contrary to popular belief, is dynamic. Even in a grain of sand the atoms perform constant pyrotechnics that would make a professional juggler green with envy.

So Life is static. It becomes manifest in the universe as vibrations. Since everything in the dualistic worlds goes in pairs, Life's co-attribute is Consciousness. Like Spirit – Consciousness is omnipresent. It permeates the universes and beyond. However, like Life, without a vehicle, It is static. It IS.(4) In order to become dynamic, It also needs a vehicle. This need is made possible by yet another divine attribute called Soul, which enables It to individualize Itself. There is but one Soul, but It can individualize itself in diverse forms. Some are able to perceive an individualized soul as light. Light, as an aspect of the Universal Consciousness, can be regarded as the source of all knowledge.

So when all is said and done, Spirit needs us as much as we need the Spirit. Without us, It just IS. With us, It becomes dynamic. It, the Spirit or Life, continually experiments with innumerable diverse forms. The more complex the form, the greater Its self-awareness or Its state of consciousness.

Isn't it fun? No wonder soul is a happy entity!

When souls first became incarnate, they are quite ignorant in the matters of creation. The individualized states of consciousness (souls) are like innocent kids being given a Ferrari. They have no *worldly* know-how; they don't know how to drive it. However, being immortal, souls can assure their own evolution by coming back, again and again, to gain knowledge, to become better drivers. *Each lifetime is the sum total of all previous incarnated selves.*(5) Ultimately they win so many races that they don't have to come back at all. Luckily for us, the advanced souls are so enamoured with racing that, more often than not, they return, just to teach us the tricks of the trade. Let us not forget that there are countless "us" on countless planets, in countless galaxies – perhaps countless universes. We need all the help we can get.

The mind is to the soul what Ferrari is to the racing driver. It is that through which the soul manifests its creative power. Contrary to popular belief, it is not the spirit but the mind and the ensuing thought patterns that are the building blocks of the universe. Spirit generates ideas—thoughts convert them into tangible reality. In the realm of Cosmic Consciousness, all attributes are beyond the limitations of time and space. They can be thought of as vibrating at the velocity of light. Such vibrations *must be slowed down*, to become perceptible in the material worlds. Slowing down of lumenal vibrations results in the *acceleration* of relative time.(6) We see the results of our efforts sooner. And here we have the crux of the matter, the fundamental purpose of the exercise: through *reincarnation into the material worlds, our learning process is vastly accelerated.*

Yet, within the worlds of slower vibrations, perfection eludes us. There is a snag, a very present danger. As Life becomes individualized in almost limitless diversity, Its components seem to forget that they are all indivisible parts of the Whole. This painful illusion leads to introversion and, ultimately, selfishness. Cayce, the Sleeping Prophet quoted above, called this condition mankind's *only* sin.(7) Selfishness or ego, is what keeps up apart; love, incidentally, is what joins us together. Periodically, more advanced souls return to earth (and other planets in other systems), to remind us whence we came. We call them saviors, prophets, even gods.... We elevate them onto our altars, but we do not really believe them. That's our second error. Because once we remember our origin, our problems are over. We rediscover the paradise which Adam and Eve left so long ago. Strangely enough, it was always there. Or here. Within us and without us.

All we must do is remember.

***
970817

FOOTNOTES

    1. Compare: According to your faith be it unto you in Matthew 9:29, also see Hebrew 11:1.
    2. Compare Psalm 82:6, John 10:34
    3. To differentiate it from a biological infestation, I shall spell It with a capital L.
    4. compare I AM THAT I AM, or I AM, Exodus :14
    5. Cayce, Hugh Lynn (editor) THE EDGAR CAYCE Reader 2. [Warner Books Edition, © 1969 by Association for Research and Enlightenment, Inc.].
    6. See Albert Einstein's theory of relativity.
    7. Edgar Cayce ibid.

8
THE QUESTION OF SUICIDE

When faced with the alternative of compromising his beliefs, Socrates unflinchingly drank poison hemlock. Did the fact that he was condemned to death absolve his action? Buddha ate tainted rice, fully aware of the consequences. The kamikaze pilots are believed to rise directly to paradise. The Moslem and the Christians also reserve this reward, each for their own martyrs: even for the premeditated, fully aware of the consequences of their actions martyrs, who died fighting, killing, murdering... on the opposite sides of a theological argument; for the countless martyrs of the "Holy" Crusades, the Jihäds. For martyr-knights, their hands covered with blood, serving *their* gods.

Are we masters of our bodies?

Are we the sole owners of the biological constructs through which we find our expression? Most of us agree that once we come of age, we are, or should be, responsible for the maintenance of our bodies, for keeping them in a good working order. This leads us to question whether we *are* our bodies (senses, minds, and emotions), or are the bodies merely temporary receptacles for our immortal selves. Once again we return to the most fundamental question of our existence: who are we?

If we identify with the physical body then the answer is clear. Anyone who witnessed humpback whales feed on whole schools of fish; who saw salmon fight its way up river (towards its spawning pond) only to be shredded by bears readying for idle hibernation; who saw Alaskan wolves tear apart live caribou... Anyone who heard of masses of lemmings' plunging headlong into the sea... Anyone who observes the world can have little doubt about nature's attitude towards killing. If we identify with nature, than we have a right to kill and be killed, by other's or by our own hand.

Yet...

Surely, whenever we kill that which we have not created we commit murder. Regardless of circumstances. To protect our wives, our offspring, or in self-defense. Murder is murder. When we kill we act like animals. Pure and simple. It is not necessary to justify our acts. Hitler never justified his murders. Nor did Stalin. Some tried, after dropping the A-bombs over Hiroshima and Nagasaki. They failed. The carnivores live according to the dictum: kill or be killed. Like the wild beast of Africa, Alaska, Europe, America, Asia, or the Middle East.

But what if we are not *just* animals?

Some of us have reached a transitional stage. Some of us hold true that we are intelligent beings capable of supporting higher states of consciousness. We believe that we, through no will of our own, are hosts to our souls.

If we belong to this group, unfortunately, little changes.

Surely we have a right, as hosts, to expel our guests on our terms. Why should we wait until the visitors vacate our bodies voluntarily? When they do, we'll surely die, yet they don't ask our permission before taking their leave. We can get even by committing suicide. We can tell them when to get off! Are we not masters in our own house? Perhaps this is why most major religions(1) justify murder with convoluting arguments that would make Machiavelli proud. Many religions preach that we are hosts to "our" souls...

Alas, murder is murder by any other name...

But what if we are *not* biological structures. What if we didn't invite any superior beings to enter our bodies, use us, and discard us when of no further use to them. What if we are not our bodies, emotions, our minds, our personalities? What if we are not that which we appear to be?

Then... WHO ARE WE?

Some claim that *we* are the aliens, perhaps superior (spiritual?) beings, who enter the ineptly named temples of clay (actually a few ounces of chemicals suspended in a bag of water) for reasons of our own. Some claim that *we* have created the biological constructs to further *our* own ends. Oh, we use the equipment which nature placed at our disposal. The chemicals, the sperm, eggs, a willing womb—whatever is available. In fact, we became so involved with our ongoing creative process that we begin to identify with the process itself. We terminate and replace thousands of cells each day. We rebuild many worn parts. We construct superb immunological systems to fight off other biological (bacterial and viral) forms threatening the wellbeing of our creation. We maintain balance between the mental and the emotional energy flows within our creation. You might say... we get lost in our creative act. Sometimes we lose the distinction between the creator and the created. Rather like a Method actor identifying with the role he or she is playing, to the exclusion of his own identity.(2)

Some of us are known to our hosts as souls.

A reasonable option?

What now of suicide? The body was not alive before we entered it, nor will it be after we leave it. Is this suicide? Not if we define life as *our* presence. Not if *we are life*. We, the aliens or souls, do not die. We enter our creation, our house, our transient state of consciousness, we work from within, and then we move on. If we are spiritual beings, experimenting with different biological structures, we enliven them even as gasoline enlivens the engine of an automobile. Yet a car needs a driver, a *conscious* presence. And this is what we are. The Conscious Presence. We enjoy the car while we drive it, but... there are other racers to test. When we build a new vehicle, we often take our toolbox with us: our minds and emotions. We have built those up over the ages. They help us along.

We, aliens, keep learning.

But then, there are Universal Laws.

We the Spirit, Soul, are above the law, but as we become incarnate, we must obey our own rules of material existence. We are Life, Consciousness, and we are also Beauty. The latter is a concomitant of harmony and order. If our creation is to function, certain rules must prevail. For those among us who lost track of who or what we are, a word of caution: every *single murder is suicide*. [At the elemental ground of being, we are all One]. The killer must restore the balance by being the victim. This is the Law of Karma. We don't die. We are immortal. But those of us who kill must experience the agony of (physical, emotional and mental) wrongful death. Then we continue. Learning. We can save ourselves future heartaches by respecting others' creation today. Like human bodies. Like animals. And trees. And flowers. Nothing on earth is eternal. Everything has been, and continues to be created by someone.

By an alien. Such as you and I.

And for as long as we continue to endow our creations with a sense of awareness, self-awareness, we are there to uphold it. We are its masters, yet in a way, we are there to serve it, to be its shining light. We are the Light.

It appears that whichever mode of being we accept, with our calculating intellect, we are the masters of our body. We and we alone decide whether we shall live or die.

Right?

Would we still kick the Alien out, send Him on His way? Would anyone really be proud of such an ungrateful act?

Would you?

***

970821

FOOTNOTES

1. ...not to be confused with the teaching on which they are *loosely* based.
2. An acting school invented by Constantin Stanislavsky, stage name of Constantin Sergeyevich Alekseyev, cofounder of Moscow Art Theatre in 1898. His acting method influenced such exponents as Marlon Brando.
3. see *A Horse of a Different Color*, BEYOND RELIGION, Vol. I.
4. Isaiah 9:6

...let the dead bury their dead

Matthew 8:22

9
REALITY

Millions of light-years away, discernible only by the most powerful radio telescopes, two giant galaxies traverse each other's orbits. Billions upon billions of stars, gaseous clouds, black holes, solar systems like our own, merge in a gargantuan, cosmic collision. Yet, seldom, if ever, any of the stars touch. There is no evidence of any collisions. Could it be that our telescopes fail us? Or is the reason for this gentle interstellar-penetration that the astronomical distances between the countless stars are so great that the danger of collisions is virtually impossible. The stars, travelling at absurd velocities manage to avoid each other. Space is mostly space. The stars, even galaxies are incidental. Just like atoms in our bodies.

Just like atoms in our bodies.

How many amongst us realize that the distances between the individual atoms, which comprise our physical bodies, are proportionately as great as the planets are from our sun? We, like the interstellar distances, are mostly space. If we truly believed it, *and the above is a scientifically proven truth*, we could walk through walls. Through trees and mountains. It's a miracle that we can't! So what do we believe in, instead? (1)

What is our reality?

Is reality only that in which we believe? If we all agreed that reality is different from that perceived by our senses, what then? Would our reality change?

9
REALITY

Millions of light-years away, discernible only by the most powerful radio telescopes, two giant galaxies traverse each other's orbits. Billions upon billions of stars, gaseous clouds, black holes, solar systems like our own, merge in a gargantuan, cosmic collision. Yet, seldom, if ever, any of the stars touch. There is no evidence of any collisions. Could it be that our telescopes fail us? Or is the reason for this gentle interstellar-penetration that the astronomical distances between the countless stars are so great that the danger of collisions is virtually impossible. The stars, travelling at absurd velocities manage to avoid each other. Space is mostly space. The stars, even galaxies are incidental. Just like atoms in our bodies.

Just like atoms in our bodies.

How many amongst us realize that the distances between the individual atoms, which comprise our physical bodies, are proportionately as great as the planets are from our sun? We, like the interstellar distances, are mostly space. If we truly believed it, *and the above is a scientifically proven truth,* we could walk through walls. Through trees and mountains. It's a miracle that we can't! So what do we believe in, instead? (1)

What is our reality?

Is reality only that in which we believe? If we all agreed that reality is different from that perceived by our senses, what then? Would our reality change?

Yes!

Reality changes constantly. Our reality is the accumulation of cultural postulates that we think, or believe, are necessary for our survival in the objective world.

To create objective reality all it takes is consensus. Our *subjective* reality shall always remain individual. What is beautiful to me may be ugly to you. And vice versa. *De gustibus non est disputandum*—there is no accounting for taste. But *objective* reality is only a question of agreement. And if two or three of us decide to change this reality—we can do so.(2) Again, all we need is consensus. We can create any reality we choose.

So why do so may people *choose* to suffer, to live in poverty, to blame others for their fate? It is a question of conditioning. People hate to let go acquired knowledge. Paul died daily,(3) but we are jealous of our mental baggage. Better a devil we know... All governments, be they secular or ecclesiastic, rely heavily on maintaining *status quo*. They are in power and they teach obeisance to tradition, respect for the establishment (that which had been established). Change is anathema to them. It spells danger: they, the kings, presidents, premiers, dictators, popes, bishops, chief rabbis, ayatollahs... might lose power. We might free ourselves from their influence, authority. According to Jesus, the priests know how to affect this "reality trick", only they will never share it with us, the ordinary folk.(4) We are on our own.

Yet, there is a way.(5)

We all go through a stage of being able to accept alternate realities as valid. We acquire this ability about the age of seven, and, regrettably, lose it by the time we reach fourteen.(6) Some people retain this ability—they become healers, they walk on hot coals. They are the miracle workers, the "reality trance inducers." It is my contention that the vestiges of this ability lie latent, if deep, within our psyche. All we need is a catalyst to launch us into the realm of infinite possibilities.

In order to accept the feasibility of alternate states of consciousness (or reality), we must accept that such exist. We must agree, within our own consciousness, that all is not necessarily as it seems. As it appears to be. That we, our bodies, are not solid forms—that there really is an "astronomical" distance between the atoms forming our bodies. We must accept that other realities can be as good as the one we recognize as such. Jesus, Sai Baba, many mystics walking the earth today, used and continue to use, this principle to heal the sick, to feed thousands with a few loaves of bread, to raise the dead. All such advanced beings accept that there is an Infinite Source from which one can extract and formulate any reality one wishes. Some call this Infinite Source the Father, others the Ocean of Infinite Possibilities. It is this state of mind necessary to access this Source, or to make it manifest in the objective reality, that Jesus called the Kingdom of Heaven.

Jesus was not teaching a religion. He was teaching the process.

Yet Jesus was helpless if one did not wish to cooperate with him. No matter what reality he might have been capable of invoking in his own consciousness, it remained subjective until "two or three" agreed with him. This agreement he called faith. "According to your faith be it unto you."(7) Jesus was the catalyst, but the actual reality change came from an agreement between him and at least one other person. The alternate reality became objectivized. According to the scriptures, the focal point, the *gate*(8), or the *door*(9), to the alternate realities represented by Jesus has remained open for nearly 2000 years. The gate is narrow, difficult, [*few there be that find it*](10), but it is still here for all who believe in his words: I *am with you alway, even unto the end of the world.*(11)

Does this catalytic power still work?
Only if you believe in it.

There is one other condition that must be met in order to succeed. Perhaps the most important. In our dealings with the

"Father", with the infinite source of all realities, the field of infinite possibilities, we must *eliminate all ambiguities*. We must have a single eye. If we don't, the field doesn't respond. We cannot doubt. But if we can raise our faith to be as great as a single grain of mustard...(12) then we shall never thirst, nor hunger. Physically, emotionally nor spiritually. We shall abide in a heaven, or rather, we shall rediscover the heaven within us, the state we lost when we stopped being children. We shall be as gods.(13) And later, if we no longer like the conditions we've created, we shall change them for better. For "in my Father's house are many mansions,"(14) many states of consciousness, many realities. In fact, we can pick and choose. Indeed, there is an infinite number of them. And we have eternity to explore them.

This is just one of the methods we have been given. I know it works. If yours is better, let me know. But until you do I shall continue to explore the universes.

They are too much fun to miss.

***

970910

FOOTNOTES

1. Wofgang Pauli proposed that electrons orbiting the nucleus are arranged in shells. As each shell is filled, it will not permit other electrons into its orbit. The resistive force, according to Pauli, is huge. This, apparently, is the real reason for the impenetrability of matter. As atoms are way more than 99.99% empty space, Leon Lederman shares my frustration in our inability to walk through walls. He explains the problem as follows: "In solids, where atoms are locked together via complicated electrical attractions, the imposition of your body's electrons on the system of "wall" atoms meet Paulis's prohibition on having electrons too close together." THE GOD PARTICLE [Houghton Mifflin Co. Goston New York 1993] pg.184 (Are you convinced?)

2. Matthew 18:20

3. 1 Corinthians 15:31

4. Matthew 23:13

5. John 14:6. The "way" represents the method, or in our case, a possible catalyst.

6. Ernest Hilgard of Stanford University, gleamed from EXPLORING THE CRACK IN THE COSMIC EGG by Joseph Chilton Pearce, [Washington Square Press, New York, Pocket book edition 1975]

7. Matthew 9:29

8. Matthew 7:14
9. John 10:7, 10:9.
10. Matthew 7:14
11. Matthew 28:20
12. compare, Matthew 17:20
13. John 10:34, Psalm 82:6
14. John 14:2

*When you arrive at the sea,
you do not talk of the tributary.*

Hakim Sanai
[The Walled Garden of Truth]

*There is only one religion,
the religion of love.
There is only one cast,
the cast of humanity.
There is only one language,
the language of the heart.
There is only one law,
the law of Karma.
There is only one God,
and He is omnipresent.*

Sai Baba

10
SPIRIT

People living in north-western Transvaal call themselves Ba Sotho. All things that are special to Ba Sotho have *moya*. The Polynesians call it *mana*. Both words have also been translated as wind, air, breath, spirit, soul and even life. In the Christian tradition, the Greek word *pneuma* has been translated as spirit, as had the Hebrew *ruach*, which also means wind and air. The Hebrews also have a word *neshamah*, which they translated variously as spirit or breath. Paul Twitchell(1) who wrote extensively on ancient religions, equates the words spirit and life as being synonymous, while defining the essence of soul as spirit. Thus between the Judeo-Christian tradition and some later writing attributing its knowledge to pre-Judaic scriptures, the Ba Sotho have covered all possible meanings.

But only the Ba Sotho people give us an insight into the nature of spirit itself. According to Lyall Watson(2), Ba Sotho regard *moya* as "the essence of nature itself." Dr. Watson compares their vision of *moya* to electricity, as being powerful but as having no will or purpose of its own. They, the Ba Sotho, lay no claim as to its origin and suggest that "it may simply exist." A few weeks ago a friend of mine came to see me. His eyes were shining with a new understanding. "There is no difference between spirit and matter," he said.

He reached this conclusion in 86th year of his life. Were he and the Ba Sotho talking about the same thing?

I became fascinated by the Ba Sothos' understanding that the spirit, while being the essence of nature itself, and being powerful, that it has *no will of its own*. Since all other aspects of *moya* seem to concur with, what became essentially, Western tradition, I racked my brains to find the equivalence of such a postulate in Christianity. If God is all, and God is spirit, then how come "God's" nature is so indifferent, so manifestly amoral? Tomcats eating their offspring, Praying Mantis masticating her mate, the strong invariably exploiting the weak, mercilessly, at every step of the evolutionary way. If spirit does have a purpose of its own, if it is guided by any reason, then why does it, in nature, operate simply by profusion? Could it be that the Ba Sotho people know something we don't?

Is God controlling or even influencing our lives? Does God/Spirit, think? Is He/It, intelligent, all knowing? Or are all such postulates merely the influences of the Greek Stoic philosophy(3), which so permeated the Christian faiths as to pervert the original teaching of Christ beyond recognition?

If God thinks then why doesn't He judge? We are told that the Father (God, Spirit) judgeth no man.(4) We are also told that "he maketh his sun to rise on the evil and on the good, and sendeth rain on the just and on the unjust."(5) Is that fair? It sounds pretty callous to me, *unless* the Bo Sotho were right. Unless the spirit is a powerful but indifferent energy. Unless all judgement is given exclusively to the Son. To us. To you and me. Actually, we are also warned not to judge each other, though, I believe, only as a practical measure. If we do, others shall surely judge us. And if we are part of nature, than the judgement shall be amoral, indifferent, perhaps worse. Why risk it? What we *must* judge is our own actions. We must discriminate whenever faced with a choice. Thousands of times a day. This should keep us busy enough to shy away from judging others. It seems there is a lot of practical advice in the scriptures.

Actually, judgement (discernment) is only necessary in a dualistic reality. In "Oneness" it has no *raison d'être*.

So what of *moya, mana,* the spirit?
Apparently we have an incredible, inexhaustible source of power at our disposal. It is omnipresent, operates by profusion, is completely amoral, non-judgmental. It acts as leavening. A little spirit goes a long way. But we must beware. The access to it is not limited to the good, the holy. Certainly not to the churches of any persuasion. To use the words of J. C. Pearce, "the leavening is ontological, neutral, impersonal, natural. God is the function of leavening, not the capacity for choosing types of leavening."(6)

***

So here we are.
It feels rather like being left to hang out and dry on our own. What happened to this kindly, old, bearded figure we all thought of as our Father? What happened to the chosen people, the elite? Will the rain really fall on all of us? Shall we all bask, equally, in the life-giving sun? Was Jesus wrong? Actually, late in his life he explained the apparent mystery. He admitted that he and his Father are one. What he could not explain to his people, at the time, is that his Father, the immortal aspect of his nature was, is, and ever will be his Higher Self.

The Ba Sotho know that there never was an "external" father figure. They, the tribal primitives, knew that adulthood consists of standing on one's own feet, taking responsibility for one's actions, blaming no one, not even the Big Ju-Ju in the sky—the name we, the advanced race, so condescendingly assign as their divinity. The Ba Sotho know of the power of the spirit. I strongly suspect they also know that we, human beings, are meant to reach out for this incredible power, that we are to use it kindly, with discrimination, for the good of all. Otherwise, this amoral power will corrupt us. Power always does. Perhaps the Ba

Sotho were not primitive at all. Perhaps we have degenerated.

God only knows, and He apparently is impersonal and amoral. Good luck!

***
970912

FOOTNOTES

1. Twitchell, Paul SHARIYAT-KI-SUGMAD [Illuminated Way Press 1978].
2. Watson, Lyall LIGHTNING BIRD [Hodder and Stoughton Ltd, Great Britain. Coronet edition].
3. Zeno (308 B.C.) taught submission to the divine will by which all things are governed. [Apparently the idea later picked up by Islam].
4. John 5:22
5. Matthew 5:45
6. Pearce, Joseph Chilton THE CRACK IN THE COSMIC EGG [Washington Square Press, New York].

To see a world in a grain of sand
And heaven in a wild flower,
Hold infinity in the palm of your hand
And eternity in an hour.

William Blake

11
THE GOOD OL' DAYS

Many, many years ago, there was a Golden Age. Adam roamed Paradise without a care in the world. But that was a *very* long time ago. The fundamentalist biblical experts place it at some 4000 B.C..

Other scholars reach considerably further back. Researches have substantiated a line of sixty-one Egyptian kings before the days of Moses.(1) But even this claim of orderly civilizations preceding the Torah by many thousands of years is puny compared to the antediluvian ages, which are counted in *kalpas* or *yugas*. According to knowledge which predates any real or imaginary kingdoms, the twilight of the first Golden Age began at the onset of the Maha-kalpa, the Grand Age(2), which lasts some 4,320,000,000 years.

The ancients believed that God breathes out and breathes in. No one knows what happens at the intake of the divine breath. But as God breathes out, the universes are formed. We, souls, populate these universes. In the beginning, we are so close to our creator as to bask in His glory. We are truly in His image and likeness. We are incorporeal, even as man was incorporeal until God formed him out of the dust of the ground and called him Adam.(3) No wonder the ancients called it the Golden Age.

The androgynous man must have greatly enjoyed his sojourn on earth. His possibilities had been limitless, his responsibilities—none. We share a semblance of this state as little children, up to the age of five or six. We are all carefree. Everyone a wonder-child. We are equipped with intuitive, or body-knowledge, which, within limits, assures our survival. We learn by direct cognition, we formulate relationship with the outside world. Regrettably, we are as innocent as we are ineffective. We are perennial takers. We don't contribute in any way. What is more, we must rely on our parents.

Under our parents' influence our reliance on body-knowledge(4) dissipates as we progressively substitute words, semantic symbols, for direct cognition, even as Adam "had been taught" to name various animals. By the time we are six, we can recognize abstract concepts. We know what the word "mother" means even without seeing her face.

We continue to drift away from the singularity of existence. We begin to recognize our four-fold nature.(5) We recognize that we are not just abstract concepts of awareness, but have at our disposal our minds, our emotions, our physical envelopes. Just like Adam, we reach for the tree of good and evil, and descent into a dualistic reality wherein we learn judgement and discernment. But not all is lost. For the next few years we retain the ability to reach back, to catch the rays of light, of knowledge, seeping through the cracks of the world we are now creating. On occasion, when our parents are not looking, we reach into Paradise, pull out a strand of gold, rejoice in the carefree existence we are now leaving behind. But rarely... Primarily we are busy building our own image of the world. We must—in order to survive in a world created by our elders. No matter how false their reality, it is the only reality we have. If we don't join it, we shall perish.

At this stage of our development, time is of no consequence. We play, we rejoice. We pack experiences to last us a lifetime. Adam's successors are said to have lived close to a thousand years during their silver age. Ours is over by the time we are twelve.

We enter the Bronze Age.

Teen-years are saturated with words. Unwittingly, we are constructing a semantic wall between us and Paradise. We sense, intuitively, that the reality we are creating is false. We rebel against practically everything. We rebel against the lies we are fed by our elders, yet, in order to survive, we learn to lie also. Soon, we no longer perceive things as they truly are. We are no longer capable of recognizing the perfection of God's creation. We lose the ability to tell the difference between the real and the illusory construct of our own thoughts, opinions. Some of us survive to pursue (usually unorthodox) inspirations. The rest of us develop allegiance to the culture in which we must live in order to survive. Survival is all, in a universe that we are taught is hostile. The final fallacy—we are taught to fear death.

The Iron Age sets in.

We are now convinced that the world we have created with our cultural conditioning is the true reality. We are no more capable of regarding it with the innocent gaze of a child than to experience it with our long-lost body-knowing. The intuitive confidence of being "one" is gone. One with our own true nature, one with the whole world. We are now alienated from that which used to be ours. We assume a defensive posture. Our world-view is now based on fear. We live in a hell of our own making in which we fear our enemies, our future; we fear for our health, lives; we fear our leaders, politicians, tax-men, police, gangsters, priesthood. If we don't obey their dictates, we shall be drawn and quartered, go to jail, lose all our possessions, or at best—we shall suffer "eternal damnation." Our life is a story of continuous anxiety, anguish, and stress. We fear what is, what might be, we fear the unknown. We fear just in case. We fear what we think is real, and what is imaginary.

Yet, in this age of Kali, the age of spiritual decadence, the only thing we should fear is fear itself.

According to the ancients, the Iron Age has been mercifully shortened to a mere 432,000 years. For us, adulthood seems to stretch forever. Time flies *only* when you're having fun. The age of drudgery, taxes, wars, struggles, obeisance, followed by the inadequacies of old age, diseases, pains—with our back ever in the yoke of civilization, the culture we adopted and helped create. We long for something we have lost a long, long time ago. But are afraid to reach out... always afraid...

Must it be so?

Partially yes. We must understand how objective reality works in order to survive within it. We must know how others think in order to communicate with them. But if I were to tell people that I spend most of my time in my magic garden, that I share their reality but do not consider myself to be part of it, I would soon become a candidate for psychiatric treatment or, at best, I would be considered eccentric.

So I will not tell you that...

I will also not tell you that I have spent most of my life intensely amusing myself, and being richly rewarded for my fun. I will not tell you that the movement from the known to the unknown, the usual process of learning, does not fill me with anxiety but with joyful expectation. I will not tell you that I live in a wondrous world filled with plethora of everyday miracles. I will not tell you that when I am alone, at the hub of my own world, in the stillness of my heart, my childhood years are as real to me now as they were, had been, way-back-when... in the good ol' days.

I will not tell you any of this.

Even though it's magnificently true.

***
970915

FOOTNOTES

1. Blavatsky, H.P. ISIS UNVEILED [Theosophical University Press, California 1988].

2. The Hindu scriptures divide the Maha-kalpa into Maha-yugas, which divide into four lesser yugas as follows: the Golden Age, Satya-yuga lasts 1,728,000 years; the Silver Age, Trêtia-yuga 1,296,000 years; the Bronze Age, Dvâpa-yuga 864,000 years; and Iron Age, Kali-yuga 432, 000 years.

3. Note: in Genesis 1:27 God created an androgynous man in his own image. In 2:7 God formed Adam out of dust and breathed life into a material form, i.e. no longer a purely spiritual being.

4. There have been many speculations on the nature of "body-knowledge". It seems to be innate, perhaps genetic information equivalent to instinct, which is stored over millions of generations in our cells. The metaphysically inclined might refer to it as soul, the subconscious, the Hebrew *nephesh*. Body-knowledge, if allowed, takes over in moments of extreme danger.

5. In Genesis 2:11 the river splitting into Pison, Gihon, Hiddekel and Euphrates symbolize this split of our single nature into spiritual, mental, emotional and physical states of consciousness. The Revelation of John echoes this concept in the parable of the four horses (of the Apocalypse).

The most incomprehensible thing about the world is that it is comprehensible.

Albert Einstein

*Imaginary time may sound like science fiction
but it is in fact a well-defined mathematical concept.
...for the purposes of the calculation
one must measure time
using imaginary numbers...
This has an interesting effect on space-time:
the distinction between time and space
disappears completely.*

Stephen W. Hawking
A BRIEF HISTORY OF TIME,
[Bantam Books, 1988 page 134].

*Time present and time past
Are both perhaps present in time future,
And time future contained in time past.*

T.S. Eliot

12
WUNDERKIND

At first sight, this German word suggests a wondrous, perhaps a wonderful kind of person. In a way, this mistranslation rings true. What the Germans call *Wunderkind*, the French *prodige d'enfant*, the English refer to as a wonder-child, a prodigy. The *Wunderkind* is both, wondrous and wonderful, and sometimes extends well beyond our definition of a child. The concept is known to many, perhaps all nations. Yet, if it is so common, so universal—where are they all? What happened to them, the wondrous children of such promise? What have we done to them? With them?

As adults, we communicate with each other in a shattered, disjointed manner. We rejoice in every opportunity to cleverly dissect and analyze images we receive with our senses, only to piece them together, again, in an arbitrary fashion, with images *familiar* to us. Next, we chop our own fabrications once more into countless disjointed fragments, convert the results into words, and finally, with great difficulty, we synthesize them into reasonably ineligible sentences. We might call this process the semantic conversion. It is as useful, as accurate, as a blind man attempting to describe a painting inspired by Beethoven's symphony to a man born deaf. We invariably insist, however, that our description or interpretation of whatever event or concept is the right one, that we hold a goodly handle on objective reality.

The images that our children receive are quite different.
A child is not born with an ability to convert his awareness of the world to a semantically-fragmented interpretation. This comes gradually, at the rate at which the

child masters control over his language. Like us, the *wunderkind* also employs his senses to define the objective reality, but in addition, he retains an inherent contact with "Eden" from which he is gradually emerging.(1) In Eden, there are no languages, no words, no sentences. There are no analytic/synthetic processes that dilute and pervert the intensity and integrity of images that the psyche receives. Jesus did not describe or even visualize the biological processes, which the blind man's eye must undergo in order to see, but rather he "beheld" a perfect eye in lieu of the blind one. A whole, complete, perfect eye. When Mozart "heard" a composition, he did not hear it as individual notes. He "heard" it all simultaneously, in its entirety. Einstein did not "see" equations scribbled haphazardly on a blackboard, but spoke of visual images, of "muscular" concepts expressing the workings of the universe. Both, he and Mozart had to spend innumerable hours, later, transcribing or converting these images to a linear interpretation. Words, numbers, even musical symbols are all linear patterns, whereas the Edenic reality is, to say the least, three-dimensional. The images we receive from Eden are non-verbal, *gestält* structures or patterns, symbols or events. They also seem independent of the confines of time or space.

Our culture demands that we convert such integrated realities into linear projections. Perhaps that is why people who have never experienced the "whole", have great difficulty in accepting its existence. They assign to the concept some mystical, religious values, esoteric mambo-jumbo, little realizing that as children we all went through a phase of having access to this undifferentiated reality. Then, as now, we need not recognize it as anything special, unusual or sacred. If, as children, we were capable of assigning semantic value to this reality, we would consider Eden our home, our inherent right.

And it is. It is our kingdom.

We, adults, are the creators of the semantic reality. We spend all our efforts in cutting the link our children have with the Edenic continuum. (J.C.Pears calls this process acculturation).(2) Having lost it ourselves, we demand that our children do likewise, or else... Later, some of us try hard to retrace our steps over this tiny isthmus. Regrettably, there is no way one can put an oak-tree inside an acorn. We cannot *go* back to this state, no matter what we do. It is the "going" or the "doing" itself that cuts the umbilical chord between us and Paradise. The best we can hope for is to empty our skins of old wine and do nothing. Nothing at all. We are told to "be still and know that we are gods".(3)

Yet there have been, surely still are, people, who retained partial or even more substantial contact with Eden. In case of Einstein, only his intellect entered the field or the continuum, whereas Jesus, when walking on water, or Father Pio, when appearing simultaneously in his monastery in Italy and in South America, actually entered the field itself. Such examples are usually relegated to "religious" experiences.

Apparently, in order to gain entry to Eden(4), to partake in the field of infinite possibilities, we must be willing, at least temporarily, to suspend the objective reality that we took such pains to create. We must be willing to give up all the accumulated knowledge, all that which constitutes our personality; in a way we must die in order to come to life within the continuum. Jesus tells us that we might succeed if we are willing to be in this world but not of this world.(5)

The reason why we cannot remain as children forever is that a prodigy finds himself in a mode of acceptance of the continuum in an open or unconditional way. Only mature individuality, such as that of Jesus, can survive in our society while maintaining substantial contact with the Edenic state of consciousness. A mature individuality allows for the *gestält* "impressions" to be sifted through the lenses of objectivity and integrated into our tangible universe. I suspect some Zen masters, perhaps great poets, artists, and some child prodigies, who have not lost their "innocence," share the privilege. Others must sever the link or end up in a lunatic asylum.

But not all is lost. Infinity is in love with time. We are the instruments through which the infinite finds its expression. And there are as many ways of expressing the infinite as there are people with courage. We cannot control it, but we can submit to the potential within us. While we continue to distort reality with our puny egos, our prodigious abilities quietly grow, mature, develop. One day we shall learn to enter the continuum with ease. This, and this alone, is evolution. All else is just walking in ever decreasing circles.

When Jesus advocated that we be like little children(6), he did not suggest that we start having tantrums, become inadequate in the performance of our tasks, lose the ability to act as adults. Becoming like a small child simply means to become whole. As adults we suffer from a self-induced dichotomy. We have accepted the duality of our world to the exclusion of any other reality. We must stop doing that. We must stop doing. We must be. Every child is a prodigy. A wonder. And within the heart of every single one of us there is a carefree, joyful, trusting child. If we stop shackling it with our conventions, traditions, customs, political and religious systems, perhaps the child will emerge, once again, to play in the field of infinite possibilities. Perhaps.

It is up to us. Up to you and me.

***

970920

FOOTNOTES

1. I use the pronoun "he" generically. The exact same applies to every young "she".

2. I owe a great deal of the material for this essay to Joseph Chilton Pearce, the author of EXPLORING THE CRACK IN THE COSMIC EGG. [Washington Square Press, New York].

3. compare Psalm 46:10.

4. Eden, Paradise, continuum, the field of infinite possibilities are all treated as synonyms. They all represent the unchangeable, undifferentiated reality which Jesus called the kingdom of heaven.

5. John 17:14 - 16

6. Matthew 18:3

13
ONE

I and my Father are one.[1] There can only be one infinity. If there were two, one would limit the other. The problem with infinity is that it's infinite. Any adjective we attach to the idea tends to limit that which is limitless. It applies equally to our concept of time and space. Just like infinity, timeless oneness has neither beginning nor end. Before Abraham was, *I am.*[2] Not being limited, means being complete. Whole. Even as there is oneness in infinity there is infinity in oneness. It is. The eternal now. The nothingness of Buddha. It is that which neither is nor isn't. Beyond definition. The I AM THAT I AM. And what is THAT I AM? It is that which Baruch Spinoza refused to define.

What of it?

The problem with many theologies is that they propound hypotheses that do not appear to have the slightest bearing on everyday life. At least, at first sight. The non-being of Buddha, the heaven within (and without) of Christ (of which, sadly, most Christians have never heard), even the Tao of Lao-tse, essentially relate to the indefinable state which is neither being nor nonbeing, nor is it even a state of eternal becoming. We might think of ourselves as being a stationary point of cognition, with the universe (the manifested life) passing us on all sides. Our bodies, minds, are part of the universe while *we* are the observers. After thousands of years, humanity is no nearer to the understanding of these, assuredly, eternal truth.

Some propose that the Avatars(3) talked about our ultimate potential, about a field of infinite possibilities, which we still fail to grasp, let alone explore. Yet, each time I reread their admonitions, I become more convinced that they all talked about the here-and-now, about the very real if timeless present. Perhaps we must reject the "objective" reality of being trapped in the eternal awagawan, the wheel of destiny. Perhaps that which creates, sustains and terminates our being, rather as Brahma, Vishnu and Siva, the divine predecessors of the Moerae, the Zeus's daughters(4), are as illusory as the Christian Trinity which came on the scene long after the Romans followed their Greek harbingers with the three Parcae, and the Norse with the Norns.(5)

With such worldly competition, it could not have been easy for Jesus to claim responsibility for his own destiny; to claim oneness with the Father, to be One. No matter, the Roman Church quickly forgot his assertion and went right back to a convenient trinity. Don't we ever learn?

I and my Father are one.
We plod, more or less successfully, through our lives, reasonably content with our lot, reasonably content with gyrating in progressively decreasing circles, knowing full-well that, barring accidents, one day we shall face Siva, who will creep surreptitiously into our creaky joints, invade our memory, devour our body and mind. We might, just might, then, in the darkening twilight shadows of our lives, make a belated, last ditch effort to find out "what of it". To ask who are we. And then, soon, so very soon, we shall be no more.

Unless...?

Unless we are also One; one with some greater whole, some inimitable oneness, which remains continuous regardless of our fleeting contribution. Unless, we too, in some indescribable manner, are one with the Father. *Follow me, I am the way.*(6)

All the way?

Do we want to be immortal? What if we get to reincarnate our consciousness into regenerated bodies (nurtured or cloned), to go through the purgatory, which, in a single lifetime, forced my father to don a military uniform and face three enemies in three bloodthirsty, rapacious, primitive wars? Love your enemies?(7) *If we were One we would only have to love ourselves.* Wars were fought thousands of years ago, they are fought today. If we are immortal, what have we learned? If we do get reincarnated, then surely we would have learned something in those countless centuries. Wouldn't we?

Wouldn't we?

Unless...

Unless life is a joke. Unless we are part of a Single Consciousness, which amuses Itself with periodically killing off the individualized containers for Its awareness, knowing that dying on the battlefield is much more exiting than the slow disintegration in a prison designed specifically for the Golden Age. I met many war veterans who count their sojourn on the battlefield among the most intense and existing segments of their lives. They were never so alive, they said, as when facing death! Some joke... or did they know something we don't? Of course we could refuse to have wars. We could love one another, instead.

Unless life is a joke...

In literature, Zen Masters always choose to behave in a crazy way. Do they too know something we don't? Perhaps to liberate oneself is to stop taking life seriously. Better still, stop taking ourselves seriously. If life is more than a biological infestation, then we are more than our exalted egos. Perhaps when we stop worrying, stop being afraid of the past, present and future, when we realize that whatever we do will not change the world one iota, then-and-only-then we shall be set free. After all, which of you by taking thought can add one cubit unto his stature?(8)

Lao-tse admonished us to stop striving. Siddharta Gautama (Buddha) claimed that our worries are but an illusion. Zen Master says: Nothing matters. Just do your best. The Christ says: Take no thought for your life, what you shall eat, or what you shall drink; nor yet for your body, what you shall put on.(9) (Nothing matters? No more diets!) Lao-tse also taught selflessness. The Buddha—compassion. Zen Masters are known for their loving-kindness. The Christ said: love one another.(10) Where did Jesus get his ideas? Lao-tse lived 600, Siddharta Gautama 500 years before Jesus was born. Did they all draw their knowledge from the same spring? From ONE source? How come none of them talked about any trinities. Were they all also One? One with the Father? Are we?

Shouldn't we try to find out? It may be worth the effort.

But if we are too lazy, then, at the very least, let us stop worrying.

***

970928

FOOTNOTES

1. John 10:30
2. John 8:58. Compare Revelation 22:13: I am Alpha and Omega, the beginning and the end... This statement "frames" infinity, in an attempt to define the integrity of oneness. Also Isaiah 44:6.
3. from Sanskrit *avatâra* descent, from *ava* down, and *tarati* he goes, passes beyond. Normally understood to be an incarnation of a deity.
4. The three Fates or the Moerae were Clotho who spun the web of life, Lachesis who measured its length and Atropos who cut it off.
5. Roman and the Norse Fates appear to have been modeled on the Greeks. Urth, Verthandi and Shuld, the Norns, spun and wove the web of life.
6. John 14:6
7. Matthew 5:44
8. Matthew 6:27
9. Matthew 6:34
10. John 13:34, 15:17.

14
NOW

I continue to be amazed how so many of my friends are willing to sacrifice the divine state of being for the illusory state of becoming. All too often they are willing to postpone living their dreams until they grow too old to fulfil them. I am reminded of a book I'd been given on my fiftieth birthday. It assured me that I am finally old enough to afford all the things that no longer interest me.

Tomorrow is another day... right?

We can't be sure. Countless alternate realities could erase tomorrow permanently, or at least alter it beyond recognition. Realities change with our perception. All it takes is two or three of us to agree, and an objective reality is manifested. We all live in worlds of our creation. I am reminded of a man who committed murder because he did not want to go to heaven. Why? Because he was very allergic to dogs. He was convinced that all dogs go to heaven.

The German philosopher Hegel(1), like the French monk de Chardin, elaborated on the evolution of a world soul. Some time ago I have written about Hegel's thesis/antithesis/synthesis dialectic which Hegel offered as a means to experience this unifying Absolute. It was a time consuming process. Teilhard de Chardin also needed time to arrive at the Omega point(2), at which, according to him, we shall achieve a certain mythical unity. Alas, time is the precondition for both hypotheses, whereas we, souls, have our being *outside* time. Any theory that takes time into consideration concerns itself with illusion, with the state of becoming. To assert my being I do not say I was nor I shall be, but—I AM.(3) This categorical precept dismisses all that is transient and affirms our immortality. Becoming, on the other hand, is *per force* a process suspended in time *and* space, and thus relegated to both transient and materialistic mode. That which has beginning must have an end.

That which is—IS.

As souls, individualizations of the Absolute, we have our being beyond time. De Chardin's Omega point already exists. Hegel's Absolute always was, is and will be. Both have their being in the eternal now. We cannot be a little divine, a little godlike. Every form of dialectic, including that proposed by Socrates, Plato, Kant or Hegel, is always part of the illusion. Dialectic is a product of the mind, and mind is transient. We, as souls, cannot become that which we already are. Soul is. How we experience the "world" (the dualistic reality) is quite another matter. Being omnipresent, we experience all possible realities simultaneously. Apparently though, we, or at least some of us, appear to manifest a need to delve into some of the realities deeper, perhaps sequentially. It is all a question of where, or on what, we place our attention.

This is where the fun begins.

We are in a speeding train with complex, gestält images flashing by the windows on both sides of our carriage. Better still, we are hovering in a weightless environment, within a starship constructed of transparent material. We don't move from our vantage point but are aware of the immensity of possible realities churning in spellbinding diversity, surely available for closer inspection. Alternatively, we remain completely static while our spaceship hurls at supra-luminal velocities through countless embryonic universes. We are the observers, the masters of the ship. Wheresoever we direct our attention, we are there.

We sense a need to participate in the realities we experience. Perhaps, one by one. There is no hurry. After all, we are immortal.

We slow down our spaceship. Nothing changes save velocity. Yet that is the fundamental change. We enter into the realm of time. First we become aware of the illusions of mind. This is what cognitive awareness becomes at lower velocities or vibrations. We are intuitively aware that in order to experience the new reality, we must identify with our vehicle (with the experimenter). We experiment with different models our mind produces and settle on a biological construct. Suddenly we are flooded with a plethora of sensations. We not only observe but, albeit on a very limited scale, we can individually participate in the dexterities of our new vehicles, the biological construct we have built. We are pleased with our effort. We call it Adam.

Life, biological life, is fun. We find great pleasure in experiencing various realities through the progressive stages of our biological development. We can experience the world as children, as adults, even as aging models. We create and enter countless epochs, civilizations, as they materialize into and dissolve from the objective reality. We enjoy drawing from our (original) Kingdom various elements, which we introduce to our new, albeit illusory, reality. We know it is not real, but... it's such fun. We all agree that the universe we continue to create is becoming more beautiful each and every day. It's like a composite echo of the infinite realm we left behind. Regrettably, all this creativity is taxing for our vehicles. In time they wear out. After all, at lower vibrations (velocities) nothing is permanent. It can't be. It is subject to the passage of time. Here today, gone tomorrow. Mu, Lemuria, Atlantis, Egypt... such fun—so transient. But we can't wait. We live only in the present and realities are infinite...

We must enjoy them while they hover on the brink of dissolution.

As the bodies we create become obsolete, we change them for new models. During the twilight of their usefulness we often leave them for extended periods to consolidate and share our experiences with other individualizations (souls) in the timeless realm. In our true Kingdom. When we leave our vehicles permanently, we revert the materials to the storehouse from which, eventually, we build new models.

Each fragment of infinity we unfold offers new challenges. Each instant, each moment we cherish as the eternal, incomparable, inimitable now. We know it will exist forever in our consciousness. It is as timeless as we are.

It's good to be immortal.

***

970930

FOOTNOTES

1. Georg Wilhelm Friedrich Hegel (1770-1831). His all-embracing hierarchical philosophy was likewise embraced by Christianity, while his dialectic is said to have been espoused by dialectical Marxism.

2. de Chardin, Teilhard THE PHENOMENON OF MAN [Harper & Row, New York 1965]

3. Compare Exodus 3:14: I AM THAT I AM, the Hebrew tetragrammaton YAHWEH. Also: John 8:58: Before Abraham was, I AM.

... what the egoless mind sees is unity.

Darryl Reanney
AFTER DEATH, *A new Future for Human consciousness,*
Avon Books, New York 1991, pg.204.
[The late Mr. Reanney was a distinguished molecular biologist, teaching at universities in New Zealand and Australia.

15
MYSTERY

The late **William F. Buckley Jr.** was known to me as an accomplished debater. Today I met him as an author. He was a guest on the Charlie Rose program to discuss his book *"Nearer to my God."* After some preliminary questions, Mr. Buckley confessed that he wanted to treat in his book some deep theological questions. Such as? "Such as the paradox of God being good, yet be so tolerant of evil." Why? Prompted Charlie Rose, Why is He. "Why...?" Mr. Buckley seemed taken aback. He recovered quickly assuming what sounded to me like a pontifical voice: "It is a Great Christian Mystery!" I added the exclamation mark and the capitals—Mr. Buckley's voice seemed to trail off...

No wonder.

Over the years, I met two types of people among the Christian flock. Those quiet, unassuming, everyday men and women who go out of their way to lend a stranger a helping hand, who willingly offer a shoulder to cry on, who reach deep into their pockets to aid those whose need is even greater. These people neither shun nor seek recognition; some neither hide nor display their clerical collar. None of this group find life a mystery—rather a marvel, a miracle, a wondrous gift to be embraced and shared.

And then there is the other group. Well situated, sedate, perpetually traditional in their outlook, just a tiny bit pompous, invariably displaying their titles, scarlet robes or other insignia of power; this latter group never fails to relegate everything they can't understand to the status of a Great Mystery. Christian or otherwise. It seem a lot easier than taking the trouble to read and perhaps even study the words on which, they profoundly assure us, rests their faith. Perhaps they are too preoccupied, too busy, with the importance of the functions they perform.

Are there really so many such great, flabbergasting mysteries? Were the scriptures written for the sole purpose of keeping us ignorant of God's intentions? Are there many as ignorant as the sheep publicly represented by Mr. Buckley? And are they really ignorant, or merely silent. *If our gospel be hid, it is hid to them that are lost*(1), claims Paul the apostle. The gospel is not hidden, and that which is not hidden is not a mystery. Isn't the very essence of the Good News that *all has been revealed?* Could it be that some seeds fell on deaf ears?(2) Perhaps the mysteries are not really Christian but form part of some other teaching.

As we live, learn, observe with open minds, surely the haze slowly dissolves.

For some twenty years I've been inundated with mysteries. I've even spent time under the daily grind of a Jesuit college. I've been forced-fed with mysteries. The mystery of the Holy Trinity, the mystery of the Virgin Birth, the mystery of the Incarnation, the mystery of Transubstantiation, the mystery of Immaculate Conception, Transfiguration, Ascension, Assumption, Resurrection, the mystery of the Original Sin(3), the mystery of Infallibility(4), the mystery of the Seven Sacraments, the... whatever-I-can't-understand mystery. Could it be that long before the introduction of Papal Infallibility, during the first eighteen centuries of hierarchical conformity, there might, just might have been some basic teachings misinterpreted at the outset and then religiously built into a conservative tradition? The Gnostics thought so and were unceremoniously destroyed by bishop Irenaeus who was never proclaimed infallible.(5) Could his zeal have been misguided, as were other fervors manifested in the Crusades(6), inquisitions(7) and other deviations(8) from the teaching of Christ?

Just for a change, let us take a look what the Bible has to say about mysteries:

Matthew 10:26: *...there is nothing covered that shall not be revealed; and hid, that shall not be known.*
Mark 4:22: For *there is nothing hid which shall not be manifested; neither was any thing kept secret, but that it should come abroad.*
Luke 12:2: For *there is nothing covered, that shall not be revealed; neither hid, that shall not be known;*
Luke 8:17: For *nothing is secret, that shall not be made manifest; neither any thing hid, that shall not be known and come abroad.*

Enough? There is more...

Matthew 13:11 ... *it is given unto you to know the mysteries...*
Mark 4:11: Unto *you it is given to know the mystery of the kingdom of God...*
Luke 8:10: Unto *you it is given to know the mysteries...*

The last three had been directed at the initiated. Were there none initiated since the apostles? Not one? To quote Matthew once more: he that has ears to hear let him hear.(9)

One cannot blame the blind for not being able to see. And mysteries are such enticing lures. Let's face it. Already Paul, in his letters, dangled the sweet scent of mystery in front of the disciples' noses. John went even further in his Revelation. But surely, Paul's letters and the Revelation of Saint John the Divine are still veritable mines of information. All one needs is to accept that the scriptures used symbols to protect the wisdom from those not yet ready to receive the gift of the Good News. *But that was nearly two thousand years ago!* Isn't it time to open our eyes?

The silent majority of Christians will not be fooled much longer. They will not believe that, after so many centuries, there is not one man speaking for the church who has been initiated into the "mysteries" referred to by Matthew, Mark and Luke. That not one man has been chosen to explain to the all-too-gullible, perhaps too obedient, sheep that *there are no mysteries*. Perhaps those in power know that the knowledge of truth will set us free.(10) Or perhaps they know, but refuse to cast pearls before swine, lest we trample them under our feet.

***
971017

FOOTNOTES

   1. II Corinthians 4:3
   2. Matthew 13:9 and six preceding verses.
   3. According to Matthew Fox, a catholic priest, St. Augustine invented the Original Sin in 4th century AD. The concept does not exist in the Bible or in the Jewish faith.
   4. Introduced at the Vatican Council in 1870.
   5. Saint Irenaeus (c.125-c.202), Bishop of Lyon, expounded in his AGAINST THE HERESIES against
   6. Nine crusades from 11th to 14th cent. The 15th – 16th cent. crusades against the Turks were also sanctioned by the pope.
   7. The medieval began c.1233 and continued into the 19th cent., with judicial torture. The Spanish established in 1478, abolished in Spain in 1840. In 1542 Pope Paul III assigned the medieval Inquisition to the Holy Office where it continues to this day (censorship, Index, etc).
   8. Such as active participation in many wars (since the crusades), amassing of incalculable riches, countless cases of sacerdotal abuse of authority in schools and orphanages and their subsequent attempted concealment and whitewashing, etc.
   9. Matthew 11:15
   10. John 8:32 and Luke 11:43 & 52

16
MIRACLES

Reality is a question of agreement. Whatever conforms to the accepted model of our universe we regard as real. What doesn't, we consider a miracle. Objective reality is that which we can define in a semantic way. For the purpose of this discussion, let us regard subjective reality as the opposite of the objective reality, i.e. a realm that is privy only to an individual, and thus different for every person. Hence, there are as many subjective realities as there are people in the world.(1) In my essay on REALITY (hereinbefore #9), I quoted Jesus as saying, "in my Father's house are many mansions,"(2) many individual states of consciousness. The sum total of all such realities Jesus called the Kingdom of God. It was also his contention, that under certain circumstances, we can gain access to this Kingdom.

Every element of the objective reality has been, at one time or another, brought out of the subjective reality. The invisible became visible. That is why Jesus assured us that, the Kingdom (continuum, heaven) is within you and without you.(3) Every objective form already existed as a potential, before it became materialized. The psalmist speaks of the same process in his uniquely poetic fashion:

> "My substance was not hid from thee, when I was made in secret, and curiously wrought in the lowest parts of the earth. Thine eyes did see my substance, yet being unperfect: and in thy book all my members were written,

which in continuance were fashioned, when as yet there was none of them." (4)

Converting the subjective into the objective states is the substance of miracles. The precondition to this occurrence is an agreement as to the substance of the event or object.(5)

The miracle must be *accepted* before it becomes "real".

Things that would have been considered miracles only a few years ago are commonplace today. Compared to our forefathers, our objective reality is beset with such luxury as to be regarded miraculous. Think of central heating and a/c, of stereo and TV, of changing winter for summer within of few hours spent sipping wine aboard a jet, of thousands of labor saving devices, which enhance the quality of our objective or *biological* life. All these inventions originated as miracles. They all had their birth as an idea that entered the consciousness of someone who, for an instant of eternity, gave up allegiance to objective reality. He was willing to accept that other realities are just as good. He touched the Infinite Field of Possibilities without preconditions, without demands, just offering himself with all his talents, faults, strengths and weaknesses. While Jesus apparently achieved this interaction on an ongoing basis, most of us can hope to experience it only on fleeting occasions.

To reiterate, the universal is the sum total of all possible subjective realities, coexistent in a single continuum (God is one). Yet the universal can only manifest itself through the means we, you and I, place at its disposal (our skills, abilities, attributes). We are the way, the means, through which the universal enters the objective world. In spite of that, we seldom have any control over how it will manifest itself through us. Usually, great paintings only "happen" to great painters; great music only to great musicians; great scientific discoveries, to great scientific minds. But the universal accepts no rules. Arigo, the Brazilian healer was a peasant. One day, he emerged from a profound trance with the ability to cure an estimated million-and-a-half patients.(6) Generally, though, the more skills we make available, the greater our chance of becoming a channel for the universal.

The Field is accessible to all, regardless of their moral or ethical standing.

The Field is non-judgmental. Contrary to many misunderstood quotations from the Bible, the Christ assures us that: "The Father judgeth no man, but hath committed all judgement unto the Son."(7) You, we, are the sons/daughters. We must discriminate in our thoughts and actions in order to survive in the objective reality. [We are warned, however, not to judge another: "Judge not, that ye be not judged."(8) We can safely leave retribution to the law of Karma.]

Do religions have anything to do with any of this?

Krishna, Lao-tse, Buddha or Jesus had naught to do with any laborsaving devices (nor with any religious rites). They were concerned with teaching us how to live in order to attain contact with the continuum. They all taught us how to live, not how to die. They were concerned with the state of our consciousness. Fasting, praying, beseeching, begging, pleading or self-denial will not get us into the continuum. It might give us ulcers or indigestion but not heaven. Buddha discovered this the hard way. Jesus called for us to enjoy a carefree life, filled with joy. We are given diverse talents, we are to use them, enjoy them. After all, as we sow, so shall we reap.(9) Let us sow joy.

But we are to remain vigilant. Single-minded.

We never know when we might be chosen. To enhance our chances, we should practice silence. We must still the stream of consciousness, or what Pears calls the roof-brain chatter.(10) I tend to think of it as a subliminal noise or simply head noise. If we succeed, we achieve the state that the prophets called Jerusalem. The city of peace. It is a state of consciousness characterized by sublime serenity, a reality beyond time and space. Only there can we attain to where our true Self resides. It is everywhere and nowhere. Krishna declares: "I am the Self, seated in the hearts of all creatures. I am the beginning, the middle, and the end of all beings."(11)

Jesus reiterates, "I am Alpha and Omega: the first and the last".(12) And then the final union: I and the Father are one.(13)

Once in this state we become one. The duality we begat in Eden is no more.

We become as gods—the miracle makers.

***

971007

FOOTNOTES

1. Not to mention the incalculable number of other intelligent entities inhabiting countless planets in countless solar systems suspended in countless galaxies.
2. John 14:2. Let us remember, Jesus spoke to men and women who could neither read nor write, and who imagined that stars are little points of light circling the earth.
3. THE GOSPEL ACCORDING TO THOMAS, logion 3. [Harper & Row, © E.J.Brill 1959]. Also refer to Kapuscinski, Stanislaw THE KEY TO IMMORTALITY (Inhousepress 2001, eBook 2009).
4. Psalm 139:15-16.
5. Matthew 18:19, 18:20.
6. In 30-second operations he "repaired" cardiac disorders, re-attached displaced corneas, removed tumors, all with the aid of a pocket knife.
7. John 5:22
8. Matthew 7:1
9. Galatians 6:7
10. Pearce, Joseph Chilton EXPLORING THE CRACK IN THE COSMIC EGG [Washington Square Press, New York]
11. BHAGAVAD GITA, 10:20
12. Revelation 1:11
13. John 10:30

17
CRITICAL MASS

In physics, a **critical mass** determines the amount of fissile material needed to maintain a nuclear chain reaction. In both math and physics the word critical denotes the stage of transition from one state to another. We know that a single exposure to viruses can exceed our organism's capacity to put up adequate defenses. The number of viral or bacterial contaminants may be said to have reached a critical mass. The many (cells) are profoundly affected by the relatively few, sometimes with deadly consequences.

Other influences of a critical mass are harder to discern.

Just two or three glances at a beautiful woman can leave a disturbing imprint on a man's emotions. He may toss and turn for many-a-night, before the effects of a critical exposure abate. I'd also aver the adage that a (single) pen is mightier than (many) a sword. Our perception of the physical, emotional and mental realities are subject to the powerful influences of critical mass. How small the catalytic mass must be is subject to speculation.

All evolutionary changes are the direct results of either a crisis brought about by a critical condition(1), or by a relatively small segment of the human race having reached a critical mass.(2) While periods of stasis are necessary to consolidate the results of previous crises, new critical conditions awaken the human race to its inherent potential, which lies stagnant in our psychic makeup. People have known the power of the critical mass at least since biblical times.

There are many false prophets who make a comfortable living by distorting the scriptures in order to benefit from sensationalism. The bookstores are replete with assurances that the end of the world is at hand. Greedy authors quote prophet Daniel, the Revelation of John, even Jesus of Nazareth, to add weight to their raving and dollars to their bank accounts. They cite many examples to back up their juicy, piquant, pungent, overly extravagant, often coarse and vulgar claims. The end of the world is at hand, they cry. Jesus is coming to rule the world with an iron hand for a thousand years. Fire and brimstone will destroy Israel in the final battle of Armageddon. The "good" shall be whisked up in a cloud of glory [rapture(3)]—those who disagree with them (the "bad") shall suffer their just deserts. And if this were not enough, they quote later seers, stretching from Nostradamus to Edgar Cayce, to the local newspaper astrologer, and the Hollywood lady wielding her tarot cards. Those discontent with the visions of psychics, refer to other prophets of doom, from Heraclitus(4) to Velikowski, assuring us that the world is destroyed by conflagration every 10,800 years, and, presumably, not a day more. This doomsday scenario has been enthusiastically supported by other Greek "scholars", if not by combustion then by a deluge, if not in 10,800 years then at other suitable intervals. It seems that there was always money in scaring people witless. At least the Hindus give us more breathing time. They support a calendar cycles of 4,320,000,000 years.

Psychics are psychics, seers are seers. Prognostication is their business. What they invariably fail to tell us is that what they all see is their own, subjective future, not ours, and even then they see only one of many possible futures. The psychics are making an educated, perhaps inspired, guess, based on the available data. In theory, there are as many futures as there are people in the world. In practice, we must meet two conditions of critical mass to achieve a substantial change in the objective reality.

The Bible calls the critical mass—leaven.

Heaven is like unto leaven, which a woman took, and hid in three measures of meal, till the whole was leavened.(5) Heaven represents every possible reality. There are no limitations in heaven. A woman symbolizes our subconscious, our *animal soul*(6), the part of the iceberg below the surface of the ocean. The leaven is the idea whose time has come. The meal is the consciousness, which must be completely "converted" to the new idea. All creative processes follow the same pattern. An idea (from the field of infinite possibilities, heaven) enters our unconscious.(7) There it grows and expands until it reaches maturity. In the final stages of development it is converted into a semantic, linear, objective form, in which it can be shared with others.

Then, the second condition kicks in.

We need agreement.(8) In cases of "local" or personal changes to reality, an agreement must be reached with at least one other person *at the subliminal level* (or to put it in the poetic biblical language "in your heart"). In cases of concepts affecting the reality in a broader sense (like the concept of the earth being round and not flat) we need a consensus on a larger scale. We need a certain critical mass. When achieved, the rest of the world follows suit. What was originally a subjective reality becomes objective, tangible, "real". The size of the critical mass varies depending on the variance from accepted norms. But one thing is certain, a critical mass results in a predictable effect. In some ways, this is what the prophecies are made of.

Leaven always does its work.

The idea grows exponentially, until it sweeps all people willing and capable of accepting the idea. Some of us stop killing, stealing, cheating. Some of us even begin to love our neighbor. Still others learn to love their enemies. While this process continues, the masses continue on their not-so-merry way. Wars, instigated and lead by artificial puppets continue to change the artificial boundaries between artificial nations. People continue to kill for sport. Most politicians continue to live off the backs of the masses. But some of us don't. In some of us, a new reality planted in our consciousness, perhaps two thousand years ago, continues to take root.

In time the idea shall reach a critical mass.

The next step in human evolution may well be the destruction of half or more of the human race. We might decide to change from quantitative to qualitative evolution. We simply don't know. There are countless balls of dirt suspended in space, in different galaxies, spinning, round and round, just like most people's lives. But the ideas have been planted, and replanted by the few in whose psyche they matured. Perhaps, even now, they are approaching a critical mass. All we need is a little time.

One day, the ideas that we are immortal souls, that we are gods, that we are all One, shall reach a critical mass. And then we shall partake in a glorious chain reaction, as the human race takes a giant leap into the unknown.

***
971013

FOOTNOTES

1. Large meteorites, volcanic eruptions with the associated global earthquakes, or particularly powerful solar flares, could be included in such.

2. Successive global empires, or the formation of global religions belong in this category. Notably, all empires and religions gradually fall, due to the dissipation of the original idea.

3. This wonderful insight into the evolution of consciousness has been perverted for religious gains.

4. Heraclitus, 540-475 B.C.

5. Matthew 13:33

6. Greek *psuché*, Hebrew *nephesh*. Also see Eve, BEYOND RELIGION, Volume I. [© 1997, Inhousepress 2001, ebook, 2009 and 2010]

7. In biblical context, the unconscious represents the beginning, the subconscious the end product.

8. compare Matthew 19:18-20

18
THE ATHEIST

We all believe in gods.
The divine images carry many faces. They range from esoteric concepts of inspiring energy to anthropomorphic gods created by sacerdotal magicians in our likeness. Most recognize God as an infinite source, a father figure who gave us our life, maintains us, and one day shall extend our existence into some nondescript location referred to as heaven. There are some that claim to aspire to an atheistic persuasion, but we soon find that they all have objects of worship. They pay homage to money, power, art, science, nature... whatever; they all need to worship something outside their own being.

The human history is replete with gods of every possible description.

The people of India, mostly Hindus, cling to images, be it in the person of Sri Krishna, albeit residing in everyone's heart as the Supersoul(1), or Bhagavan, the Personality of Godhead. A kaleidoscope of lesser gods exceeds in numbers those of the later Greeks, though His Divine Grace A.C. Bhaktivendanta Swami Prabhupada assures us that the "demigods, being like other living entities in the material world, are all liquidated at the time of the annihilation of the material structure."(2) Not much future in that for us—simple folk.

The Egyptian theogony is as complex as that of Hinduism. People who associate early Egyptian religion with Isis and Osiris must retreat to Hermes, the Trismegistus, the god of wisdom, and the later emanations of himself. The voluptuous pantheon of the Egyptians, as of the earlier

Hinduism and the later Greeks, consists essentially of the personalized powers of the unseen universe.

Infinite universe manifests infinite powers....

The Greeks loved beauty, wars, and hunting. They loved great many things. They tried hard to deify them all. They not only personalized and idolized the invisible powers, but also the many human traits, both good and not so good. The Olympians could be as nasty as they could be nice. There was a separate god for just about every occasion.

The Romans, whose greatest accomplishment was to adopt just about everything from the Greeks, transferred the Olympus to the Pantheon and added a few animalistic quirks as well some egotistical, homicidal maniacs to their divine who-is-who.

In the meantime, the Hebrews acclaimed a single deity, and by naming it YHWH (Yod, Hé, Wau, Hé), they assigned it male and female principles, thus initiating an image of an androgynous, anthropomorphic god. Most of the time, most Hebrews, tried hard to stick to monotheism, but allowed their god to be dualistic not only in the realm of embodying the male and female principles, but by wielding the power of both good and bad. Their god rewarded and punished them with equal dexterity. But they must have missed the rich fabric of the multiple gods of other religions. Thus, instead of creating a pantheon of their own, the Hebrew developed a veritable plethora of rules and regulations, of which even the later Vatican church would remain jealous.

And then a stranger appeared.

After countless centuries of spurious demagoguery, there came a man who rejected all the man's divine creations. He rejected all gods, of all religions, which externalized the power man held within his own being. He recognized a power greater than that available to him, but then firmly placed the seat of this power within himself.(3) Finally, he affirmed that the power within, and he, are one and the same.(4) That the difference is quantitative but not qualitative. Yet, and this is vital for all of us, he did not usurp this power for himself but reminded us that it is available to all people.(5)

How strange he must have sounded after the numerous generations of weaklings grew comfortable in blaming external conditions for their station in life. They blamed the countless gods, leaders, governments, politicians and the attendant taxes, priesthood, teachers, financial market conditions, the medical profession, the environment, the weather...

Does this remind you of anyone?

Yet this one man dared to say that we, and we alone, are responsible for our lot. That as we sowed so would we reap.(6) That we, and we alone, must judge our actions, for there is no power, not even a god who would judge us.(7) He insisted that nothing is impossible for us.(8) That whatever we truly believe in, we can accomplish—but it is our belief and conviction that is the causative factor in our lives, not any external conditions.

He taught that we alone are the masters of our dominion.

***

Tough medicine.

No one to blame? No judgmental gods? No punishments and rewards? No one to be scared of? No one to bribe with gifts and sacrifices? No religion could possibly put up with such nonsense. Yet the commandment said: thou shalt have no other gods before me.(9) And he didn't. He also advocated loving our neighbors and our enemies.

So... they crucified him.

For blasphemy.

And who can blame them, the primitives of two thousand years ago. What leader of any present-day church wouldn't do the same?

***

971015

FOOTNOTES

1. SRIMAD BHAGAVATAM, First Canto, [The Bhaktivedanta Book Trust, New York].
2. ibid, pg. 129
3. Luke 17:21
4. John 10:30
5. John 10:34 and Luke 17:21
6. Galatians 6:7
7. John 5:22
8. Matthew 21:22
9. Exodus 20:3

Life is a challenge—meet it.
Life is a game—play it.
Life is love—enjoy it.
Life is awareness

Sai Baba

19
MORE ABOUT PRAYERS

There comes a time when nothing new can be said on certain subjects. The same old truths are banded again, round and round, seemingly to no avail. The various avatars endeavored to state the immutable Truth in different ways, from different points of view. Over centuries, as our consciousness develops, our perspective changes. The truth remains the same. Einstein's geometry wouldn't help in the construction of house. Euclidean wouldn't be of much use in astrophysics. But we still need houses.

Yet our points of view have changed.

Some of us travel faster than others. But in the context of eternity, sooner or later, the hare and the turtle lose their meaning. He who travels faster will spend more time in the Bardo(1), fine-tuning his findings. Ultimately, we are all part of the indivisible Whole. None can get to the finish-line leaving the others behind. In a way, we must cross the line all together. But don't hold your breath. We're immortal and—there is no finish-line. Hopefully, contrary to the misunderstood heaven of the Christians and the Moslems, infinity really *is* infinite. There are no boundaries, ends, final indisputable results. There is only the journey. The Way. The Tao. And heaven is all around us. Within and without. Within—the infinite potential; without—the trial runs, the visible segments of the invisible.

And this brings us to prayers.

As we have (hopefully) established in the previous essay entitled THE ATHEIST, the difference between "I and my Father" is quantitative. No disciple is greater than his master. The Father, the Field of Infinite Potential, is not only the sum-total of all realities already manifested in the objective world, but the endless possibilities still awaiting us, ready for us to be discovered. We, the individualizations of One Soul, have the function of converting the invisible into the visible. God, Father, the Field, has no other way of being than in a mode of being. You and I, today, are such specific modes of being. Tomorrow we might be another. Or, we may die. Not by terminating our biological functions, but by rejecting or ignoring our spiritual nature. By becoming attached to our acquired knowledge, customs, traditions, beliefs—spiritually we cease to exist. We cease to exist by becoming attached to that which is transient. Our minds become set, stagnant, unable to accept new ideas, new wine.(2) Jesus called such people dead.(3) Not because there is anything wrong with our beliefs, but because we stopped performing the spiritual function for which we have been created.

There is an infinite number of other modes of being just waiting to be manifested. God needs us as much as we need God. This invulnerable bond is called Divine Love. Only if we become aware of our potential, we become alive. *He who believeth in me, though he were dead, yet shall he live.*(4) He who believes in being an immortal soul, an indivisible part of the Whole, who knows that he or she is one with the Father, the Totality of Consciousness, who can disengage himself from physical, emotional or mental attachments, he is or becomes alive. As I never tire of repeating, Paul died daily.(5) He had to die, in order to regenerate his potential. To clean his slate. To become fully available to the transforming potential within him. This is where prayer comes in.

When we pray, we make ourselves available to the Field.

The disciple is not above his master.(6) The DNA in our fingernails is identical to that in our whole physical body. Yet the body is greater—infinitely greater, than the sum of its parts. Equally, "I and my Father are one", inseparable, but the "Father" is infinite, "I" am not. In our prayers we can make ourselves available to be used for the benefit of the Whole. To be truly alive. The Field, the Father, cannot refuse anything when faced with such an offer. After all, this is the very reason why we have been created, nurtured, developed, protected. Whatever we ask in the name of the immortal, indestructible, indivisible nature of our being, cannot be refused. There is but one condition. Since we are indivisible from the Field, we must be in total agreement with It. Any doubt closes the gap, the way through which we contact the Source. We must eliminate all ambiguity. This is the meaning of the "whatsoever you shall ask in prayer, *believing,* you will receive"(7) condition. We cannot serve two masters: the Field and our ego. The ego, with all its appurtenances, separates us from our true nature. The ego is the result, not the cause. Each one of us is an integral part of the Eternal Cause.

As we develop, we become a greater, more conscious instrument of the Whole. We forever maintain our individuality (not personality) or that which makes us unique. In time we shall be of greater use to the Field, the Father. We shall have more to offer, greater talents, abilities, techniques. The Field doesn't create these, not directly. We do, but only as part of the Field. And then we use our attributes or allow them to be used (consciously or not) to bring out the subjective into the objective reality. Not only our abilities grow, but our universe. Not only our subjective universe, our point of view, but the objective universe, as we find agreement with our neighbor. This, surely, must be the prime reason for loving (feeling oneness with) our neighbors. Without other souls in agreement, we cannot make our subjective gifts objective. We cannot make them come alive for all to share.

Without others, *we cannot grow*.

It never ceases to amaze me that this knowledge has been known and disseminated, in simplest way possible, almost two thousand years ago. The seed had been sown. Surely, by now, the human race has become a fertile soil. In the Age of Aquarius, we shall all tend our own gardens, our states of consciousness. We shall all become conscious channels for the Field of Infinite Possibilities. Let us make sure we don't forget to water our gardens with prayers, least they wither and die.

***
971018

FOOTNOTES

1. In Buddhist tradition, the hypothetical state of consciousness in which soul finds itself between reincarnations. Literally: transition.
2. Matthew 9:17, Mark 2:22 et al.
3. Matthew 8:22
4. John 11:25
5. I Corinthians 15:31
6. Matthew 10:24, Luke 6:40. Luke's version adds that though the disciple is not above his master, every one that is perfect shall be as his master. A forerunner of "I and my Father are one".
7. Matthew 21:22 (I added the italics)

Also I am ancestral. Aeons ahead
and ages back, both son and sire I live mote-like
between the unquickened and the dead—
From whom I take, and unto whom I give.

Siegfried Sassoon

20
RIGHTS

"**Rights are Rights are Rights.**"
With these words the silver-haired Clifford Lincoln resigned his seat in the Legislative Assembly of the Province of Quebec. For Mr. Lincoln, Rights were synonymous with being human. The not-so-human, not-so-liberal Liberals imposed restrictions on the freedom of their citizen to use their mother language. They made some of their citizens a little subhuman. Perhaps—in their own image.

Among the civilized societies, there are Charters of Human Rights and Freedoms, which protect the quality of our lives. Among the greatest of these is, or should be, the freedom to do the job for which we have been born. Strangely enough, there are but two objectives that define our Rights during our sojourn on earth. One, to be instrumental in *enriching the fabric of our lives*. The second, to *share and enjoy* the fruit of our labor.

This leaves us with the question of the means.

Two thousand years ago a method was proposed, guaranteeing desirable results: Whatsoever *ye ask in prayer, believing, ye shall receive.*(1) "Whatsoever" certainly sounds promising! What's more, we are assured that the source is inexhaustible. Let us examine the method in modern language: "Whenever we make ourselves available, without reservations, without ambiguities, to the Field of Infinite Possibilities, It, the Field, shall make use of us." The purpose of *receiving* is to enrich the fabric of our lives. We live in an objective universe which, though large and growing—remains limited.(2) The Field, in biblical terms the Kingdom of God, is Infinite. Furthermore, each one of us is an indivisible portion of It.(3) We are also told that Field is non-judgmental.(4) Therefore, each one of us has equal opportunity to gain access to It. All we need is a method, and that is spelled out above.

Access to the Field is a *Right*.

The Pope is said to lie prone, praying, for six to eight hours a day.(5) But praying will not (necessarily) get him, you, or anyone else to heaven. "Not every one that says to me, Lord, Lord, shall enter into the kingdom of heaven; but *he that does the will of my Father.*"(6) And "if any man will do his will, *he shall know of the doctrine...*"(7) We now know what to do and how to do it. The method has been available to us and our forefathers for two thousand years.

A word about the enigmatic "will"?

First, let us get something very clear. *No one ever goes to heaven*. Heaven is not a place; it is a State of Consciousness. No amount of prayer will assure us this state. No sacrifices, no fasting, no priestly robes, talismans, "holy" relics, crucifixes, churches, sermons, or prostrating oneself in the Sistine Chapel will assure us of this result. There is but one method to enter this State, and one only. And that is "to do the will of the Father". We are given a hint in the Lord's Prayer. I refer to the phrase: Thy *Kingdom come*. Not "take me to Thy Kingdom", nor "get me there after I die"(8) (according to the various churches, not a minute earlier). We are intended to enjoy the glory of the created, manifested, mode of being. Could it be that we can assist in bringing about this "Kingdom"? Could this be the enigmatic will?

I bet my life on it!

We are—or can be—the hands, the eyes, the ears, and the mind of God in the objective universe. We are the means through which the Infinite Potential becomes manifest. In this sense, we are gods.(9)

Our job is to bring that which is within to be without, from the inner to the outer, from the subjective to the objective. Never the other way round. We do not pray to go to heaven, but to have heaven come to us! *Thy Kingdom come!* What will happen after our death is neither here nor there (no pun intended!) No savior, no mystic, no saint ever defined the nature of our continued existence within the inner worlds. The best we can do is to assume that *all modes of being are states of consciousness.* Everywhere and everywhen. The best we can say is *"que sera, sera."*

In the meantime we must do our job.

Obviously, we cannot do the job with just our own power. Even the man, whom a billion Christians deified, by his own admission could do nothing on his own.(10) What we can all do is to offer ourselves as channels for this process. Offer our abilities, talents, skills. *Ourselves*. This is what true artists, composers, scientists, poets do. Also some mystics. We become the instruments through which heaven becomes manifest on earth. We are the instruments through which the Field of Infinite Possibilities enriches our lives, our sojourn on earth. We can ask, but we cannot dictate the results. We shall receive. Guaranteed! We must assume, unconditionally, that the Infinite Intelligence knows what's best for us. It shouldn't be too difficult. Look at the beauty of the world around you. Enjoy it. Unwittingly, you were probably responsible for some part of it coming into being. We are not to worry about tomorrow, or the day after, not to mention about our souls ending up in some illusory hell of religious zealots. Nor are we to worry about being sinners—but to rejoice in being the instruments of the Infinite. As perfect instruments as we can be. As I have written so many times, *we* are the "way" through which the subjective becomes objective.

It has been said before, it bears repeating. God has no being except in a mode of being. We don't know how many modes there are. Perhaps an infinite number. But we do know one thing. Each one of us is one of these modes. Being is our inalienable Right. And acting as channels for the manifestation of Infinite Possibilities is also our Right. And

rejoicing in the results is also our Right. And no government can take is from us. Civil or ecclesiastic.
Rights are Rights are Rights.

***
971021

FOOTNOTES

1. Matthew 21:22
2. Applying Hubble's law (D=V/k) the observable universe is a sphere with a radius of 3.4 billion light-years. Doubtless, the size will change as we continue learning. [NB: By the year 2010 radius of the observable universe had "grown" to almost 14 billion light years]
3. "I and my Father are one" (John 10:30), and "every one that is perfect shall be as his master" (Luke 6:40).
4. John 5:22
5. HIS HOLINESS by Carl Bernstein and Marco Politi, [Doubleday, New York]. This is neither in praise nor condemnation of prayer, but a comment on its efficacy. "Correct" prayer is a prerequisite for progress and evolution.
6. Matthew 7:21 (my italics)
7. John 7:17 (my italics)
8. "I pray not that thou should take them out of the world" John 17:15
9. John 10:34-35
10. "The Son can do nothing of himself..." John 5:19

21
THE ANTICHRIST

In his amusing fable *"The 1980's Countdown to Armageddon,"* Hal Lindsey allots a number of pages to the man he calls the anti-Christ. Mr. Lindsey describes him as an evil and powerful man, a leader of a coalition of ten nations. The author even claims to have an insight into this mythic anti-Christ's mind but stating (presumably with a straight face) that the man will attain unprecedented power: "the top spot in Europe on the strength of his own personality." I decided, there and then, not to go to Europe, lest I'd inadvertently fall under the spell of this prodigious and charismatic monster. Or at least to delay my trip until after the Armageddon. Then, if I understand Mr. Lindsey correctly, all would be safe to enjoy my European holidays, unless of course, I got whisked up to heaven (indicated by an upward pointing arrow on Mr. Lindsey's diagram) in Rupture.

To give Mr. Lindsey his due, he is not alone.

Both Oxford and Webster dictionaries, the Viking Encyclopedia, and who knows how many other illustrious sources, define the Antichrist as a great personal opponent, an antagonist, of Christ, a person who will lead the forces of evil. Admittedly Mr. Lindsey took the idea a bit further, but, well... he had to sell books. He counted on, apparently successfully, that the buyers of his multitudinous editions would never take the trouble to check out his sources. Nevertheless, his book boasts to have spent "over 20 weeks on the New York Times bestseller list." Lately, the source from which he supposedly concocted his story, the Bible, must have been out of fashion. Even the churchgoers seem to prefer listening to the ramblings of various sacerdotal protagonists then dig into the original, often sublime, always informative source of knowledge.

There is a veritable avalanche of pseudo-exposés of all kind, presumably precipitated by the millennium fever. Indeed, it is fashionable to talk about prophecy, to expect the worst, to scare people out of their wits. Look at the successes of all the science fiction, horror, and fantasy films, books, and cults. The more the merrier.

But what has any of this to do the Bible?

NOTHING.

Nothing at all! It's all to do with bank accounts. Pure and simple. That and peoples' inertia, mental stagnation, inability or unwillingness to make an effort on their own. They would rather someone did their thinking for them. No matter how badly.

What does the Bible has to say about the antichrist? The Old Testament—nothing. The four gospels—nothing. In the 1341 pages of my King James Version, the word antichrist occurs four times. John uses it three times in his first epistle and once in the second. Sorry folks, b-b-b-but that's all!

And how does John describe the antichrist? Why, strangely enough, as an opponent of the doctrine of Christ. As one who denies the Father and the Son. And by the way, John does not even reserve front row seats for the antichrist's appearance at the end of the world, (circa the year 2000?), but assures us that the antichrists had been walking the earth in great numbers, already, in his day. This little tidbit of information must have slipped Mr. Lindsey in the "25 years he'd been studying the prophesies". Strangely enough, it took me about five minutes to discover this trifling inaccuracy. No matter. As I said before, Mr. Lindsey is not alone.

So who or what is the antichrist?

THE ANTICHRIST

John, enjoys the distinction of having written the shortest book in the Bible. It is he who coined the word. Once again: *He is antichrist that denieth the Father and the Son.*(1) It seems quite straightforward. Not an evil leader of ten European nations but he that does not accept the concept that there is a Spiritual Reality, a Consciousness which can manifest Itself in human form. When a son raises his consciousness to manifest oneness with the Father, he becomes the Son. He manifests Christ Consciousness, or an awareness of Oneness. He can then say, "I and my Father are one." Anyone who is against this notion is an *anti*-Christ. And we are told that even in the days of John, there had been *many antichrists.*(2) Then, and surely now, there are many who deny that we are all spiritual beings. We are told that we "have" a "soul", which is a far cry from being a spiritual being, temporarily embodied in a physical shell. A far cry from having a spiritual nature.

Furthermore, we are told that even he who is an antichrist is spirit. To once again quote John, *every spirit who* denies that Christ is the spirit (of God) incarnate, is the *spirit of antichrist.*(3) Obviously. As stated above, we are all spirits (incarnate). But don't forget the Father is non-judgmental.(4) The divine traits are equally accessible to all, the good and the not so good. To the Christ and to the antichrist. Of course, the consequences of misuse or abuse of power are quite another story.

Yet there is a phase in every man's life when he (or she) is particularly susceptible to displaying the characteristics of an antichrist. It is the stage wherein his, or her, intellectual powers develop to the stage of considerable effectiveness. For a while such a person might think that he doesn't need God, that he is divine himself. After all, the scriptures assure us that we all are. If the man survives this test, the danger passes. Soon he learns that no part is greater than the Whole. He learns humility. It is then that real life commences.

It is as though he was born again.

And thus, quite contrary to Mr. Lindsey, I would respectfully suggest that there are many antichrists walking this earth today. Regretfully, great many indeed. Great many people do not accept that they are spiritual beings, that they are incarnated here for a reason. Perhaps Mr. Lindsey's time would be better spent attempting to find out what this reason is, rather then spewing fables on the unsuspecting, all-too-gullible public. I'd hate to think what John would have to say about his writings.

***

971023

FOOTNOTES

1. I John 2:22
2. I John 2:18
3. In I John 4:3 the idea is expressed in a more poetic form. Also see II John verse 7.
4. John 5:22

Show me the evil in this universe
in which no good at all is contained,
or the good in which there is not the slightest touch of evil!
...you cannot...
because good does not exist apart from evil.

Jalal-ud-Din Rumi
LIGHT UPON LIGHT, Inspirations from RUMI, translated and adapted by Andrew Harvey [North Atlantic Books, California 1996, pg.142]

22
PAIN

As **pharmacological science** advances, the antidotes for pain continue to improve. Pain inhibitors become so efficient as to interfere with our safety. After all, pain is but our organism telling us that something unusual, possibly dangerous, is taking place in our body. If we eliminate it before finding the cause, we play with fire.

But such pain is of little consequence for people of advanced mind control. A technique called biofeedback can stimulate our system to produce natural analgesics.(1) Yogis can "switch off" the neurotransmitters or conduits, which communicate the painful irregularity to the brain. Better still, since our body has a natural self-healing capacity(2), they seem to relegate all the restorative functions to the lower brain, freeing the frontal lobes to continue with conscious functions. Some of us practice the art of self-hypnosis, perhaps the first step towards the mastery over our body.(3) Hypnosis is similar to the yogic method as it enables us to bypass the judgmental capacity of our brain (that part which corresponds to our subconscious mind).

There is also a method bordering on the spiritual.

It relies on the premise that we do not have the capacity to think about two things at the same time. By diverting our attention from pain, we lose awareness of it. Spiritual awareness (reality) is virtually synonymous with *attention*. We "are" where our attention is. As we divert attention our reality changes to wherever our attention goes. As an example, even a severe cut sustained under water goes unnoticed until we become aware of it. Then, and only then, it stings.

The most advanced method of eliminating not only the pain but also its cause is spiritual.

We insinuate a different reality in lieu of that which causes the particular discomfort. Advanced spiritual beings have the ability to accept any number of realities as equally good alternatives, as objectively real. A sick or injured body in one reality is a healthy body in another. The spiritual method works best on others; the reason is that we cannot gain access to the "Field of Infinite Realities" (the biblical heaven) in a state of ego-consciousness. Whenever we enter the Field, we must leave our personality behind.

Thus, we are the masters of our fate.

Ignorance is no longer an excuse for anyone interested in mastering pain or to developing the ability to heal oneself. Most of the methods listed above are available no further than your nearest bookstore. Thereafter there is only the inseparable duo: will and work. The last method demands also faith. In fact, relies on it.

However, most such physical sufferings, or discomforts, are of little consequence. There is usually an aspirin, a stronger painkiller or, if necessary, a quiet session with oneself (self-hypnosis). The medical profession should not be ignored, but used only as a last resort. After all, we are here to learn. Perhaps that is why saints, martyrs, advanced beings, seldom experience physical pain. Perhaps their consciousness no longer identifies with their physical body in duress. The countless representations of martyrs with blissful expressions on their faces are no exaggerations. Nevertheless saints and other spiritual masters did not rise above mental suffering. To eliminate *all* suffering we must conquer time itself. And to do so we must acquire the divine trait of patience.

Patience is by far the most fundamental attribute we must acquire in order to rise above mental anguish. Patience and a full realization, an unshakeable conviction, that all things, all events, even all feelings and most ideas in this world, are transient. Given sufficient patience, we can rise above all pain. Hence patience is considered a Divine Trait. Yet no one can teach us patience. Like all divine traits, it can only be acquired by total commitment to the divine potential within us.

Picture the Christ.

After years of training under the Essenes (later in the Far East), Jesus employed not only his inherent attributes but also all the acquired expertise to pick a dozen men. A dozen apostles. The absolutely best he could find. After spending three years training them, three years of round-the-clock tuition by word, example, and spiritual influence, this pick-of-the-crop remained almost as ignorant in the end as they have been in the beginning. No matter what parables, allegories, miracles, or even direct revelation he exposed them to... alas, all to little avail.

Most of the apostles, most of the time, had but a vague idea what Christ's teaching was about. In lieu of anger or desperation, Jesus displayed virtually divine patience: "Are ye also yet without understanding?"(4) Finally Peter had gotten just *one* thing right and he was immediately appointed the leader.(5) And what did Peter do a short while later? He denied all knowledge of his Master, three times in short succession. And Peter was the (spiritually) brightest, the most enlightened, presumably the strongest of them all! As for the masses of disciples to whom Jesus dedicated his life, they too contributed to further anguish: "seeing they see not; and hearing they hear not, neither do they understand."(6) More pain. And this in spite of this incredible human being's spiritual knowledge, training, unquestionable uniqueness... wisdom and nature so advanced that some of his immediate followers attempted to deify him. Only total acceptance that all things happen in their own time relieves one, if partially, of emotional pain and mental anguish. And, once again, to achieve this realization we must aspire to, virtually, divine patience.

The lesser, the more common, everyday-type pain, is invariably the result of attachment. Usually attachment to a *status quo*. We enter a state of stasis, and when our blissful *dolce farniente,* our comfortable mindset, is threatened, we experience pain. We suffer withdrawal symptoms: physical, emotional or mental. Withdrawals of drugs, of a fickle, unfaithful lover, of an idea (loss of traditions, outdated concepts). I recall my aunt who couldn't function if she hadn't been served tea and biscuits at exactly 11 o'clock. Lao-tze advocated the escape from the illusion of all desire. Buddha taught the art of detachment. The Zen Masters say that nothing matters. Jesus told us not to worry about *anything* (food, clothing or tomorrow).

Yet Jesus, as did Socrates before him, had to face the final pain.
The pain of rejection.
Not the rejection of the teacher, but the rejection of the teaching. "How is it that they do not understand?"(7) We can't understand because we are not yet ready. We are still attached to our old ways. I can hear the great teachers saying: "I know, I know... but it still hurts..." The divine attribute of patience came to the Christ only in the very last moments of his temporal life: "Forgive them for they know not what they do."
Precisely.

We simply don't know what we are doing.

When the light finally dawns, it cannot be expressed with words, with well-modulated arguments, with philosophical dissertations. Nor with beautiful fables, parables, or even example. All knowledge comes from within. Yet, perhaps in desperation, perhaps out of equally desperate love, he who senses the light shall try to share his treasure with the select few, perhaps in simplest of words, perhaps in timid waves of compassion. Such a man will be long past any physical discomforts, any physical suffering. Nor will such a man experience any anguish of attachment to any mindset, to any desire that would limit his freedom. Yet, the pain will remain even as he cries, as so many have cried before him.... *How is it that they do not understand?*

***

971026

FOOTNOTES

1. A relaxation technique that uses electronic equipment to amplify body responses.
2. The natural analgesics are called endorphins. Our body's ability to heal itself is discussed in SPONTANEOUS HEALING by Andrew Weil, M.D.,[Balantine Books, New York].
3. SELF HYPNOTISM by Leslie M. LeCaron, Signet Book, New York 1964
4. Matthew 15:16, Mark 7:18 also Luke 2:50 et al.
5. Matthew 16:16
6. Matthew 13:13
7. Mark 8:21

*The Lord said,
James, do not be concerned for me
or for this people.
I am he who was within me.
Never have I suffered in any way,
nor have I been distressed.
And this people has done me no harm.*

THE APOCALYPSE OF JAMES
The (First) Apocalypse of James, intro. and transl. by William R. Schroedel,
THE NAG HAMMADI LIBRARY, Gen. Ed. James Robinson,
Harper San Francisco 1990, pg. 265, v.15.

23
ZEN AND THE BIBLE

There are many sects among Buddhists as there are among Christians, but most Zen Masters, as do their Christian counterparts, fall into two main categories. The first group corresponds to the Christian priests or preachers (orthodox or protestant), inasmuch as they cater to the welfare of the "masses". To this group belong all people who seemingly benefit from "sitting still and not thinking" (including participators in the broadest spectrum of meditation techniques), as well as others who prefer to subject themselves to quite demanding activities of Christian liturgy and rituals. Such would include standing, walking, sitting and kneeling during some rites, processions, pilgrimages, fasts, etc.. While silence and non-intrusiveness is practiced by some Christian monks and introverted orders, it is Zen which can be said to excel in the art of "non-doing".(1) This sentiment is expressed in Jesus' question "which of you, by taking thought, can add one cubit unto his stature?" Admittedly more Zen followers "keep still" than Christians, but this could be a matter of the secularity, which crept into the Christian churches. After all, one can hardly run a billion-member organization by doing nothing or not thinking. While Buddhists remain perfectly still, some Christians might be hard pressed to recall the origin of the words "*keep still* and know that I am God".

The very essence of Zen is being still. If one is to take into account some of the fundamental admonitions of the Old and the New Testaments, then the practitioners of Zen are much better Judeo-Christians than the Jews or the Christians.

Ideally, the sitting is done in a lotus position, a posture requiring considerable flexibility of knee and ankle joints, but after all, the Christians like to kneel, a posture even less comfortable over longer periods of time. In either case, the posture is not (or should not be) of prime importance. Chuang Tzu, a great Zen Master, summed up his method simply as "sitting down and forgetting everything". A Zen poem says: "When sitting, just sit—Above all, don't wobble". The physical stillness will, hopefully, lead the practitioner to an emotional and mental stillness, ultimately taking him, or her, beyond the subliminal noise, past the stream of consciousness. We shall become still and, perhaps then, "know who we really are."

Shunryu Suzuki Roshi said: "When a frog becomes a frog, Zen becomes Zen. When you understand a frog, through and through, you attain enlightenment; you are Buddha." I would suggest that to gain this level of understanding, we must achieve oneness, or total identification, with the object of our contemplation. The statement does not place the frog above anything else in the universe; it says that God is equally present everywhere and thus in everything. There is nothing outside God. Rather like the saying, "I and my Father are one". It cannot be otherwise. None of us can be separate from reality, and God is the sum-total of all possible realities.

Zen Buddhism might be said to lead to an attitude of unknowing. It attempts to reach back to a "beginner's mind"––knowing nothing, starting from the very beginning. "Your Father knows what things you have need of, before you ask him," comments Jesus in like vein.(2)

But there is one Buddhist trait that Christians seem to have all but forgotten.

The Zen Masters are said to like to play a fool—as though they refused to take themselves too seriously. Paul (the apostle) expresses this sentiment in his own way: "If any man among you seems to be wise in this world, let him become a fool, that he may be wise".(3) Perhaps both philosophies advocate this as an insurance against pride.

And then we have the second category.

In Zen, there is the archery.(4) This Zen category seems as incomprehensible to the Western mind as Jesus' teaching, which bears little or no resemblance to the promulgations of the organized Christian orthodoxy. This is not intended as criticism but as an observation, which can readily be substantiated by many extracts from the scriptures. In fact, as mentioned in the first paragraph, the churches have a function to play which, while differing from the original teaching, may well be more important to the physical survival of the human race. Surely, a noble cause. Jesus' teaching, however, had little to do with physical survival. Likewise, Zen archery has little to do with hitting the target. Yet the Zen Master does find his target, and Jesus claimed to be Life itself.

This type of Zen Master does not concern himself with the masses. His sole concern is to achieve oneness with, or to be taken over by, what the Christians would call, the Spirit. I understand, (no one can know for certain what happens within the walls of the monastery), the Zen Master strings the bow which no ordinary human can string, and then he waits to be "breathed" by.... to become an instrument of that-which-is. Or isn't. Zen Buddhists detest definitions. When the moment is ripe, the arrow finds its target, though that is not really the object. The Zen Masters of Archery teach their acolytes how to be by ceasing to be oneself. The Master affirms that it is not he who releases the arrow. Jesus says: "...I do nothing of myself."

And what of Christian Masters?

St. Francis of Assisi comes to mind. There must have been others. I rather think that, nowadays, they are seldom known, seldom seen. They are spiritual beings, walking the path of the Masters who came before them. They shun fame and riches, yet they never lack anything they need. Their arrows also invariably find the targets. Perhaps they really do nothing of themselves.

***

971028

FOOTNOTES

1. Zen, from Chinese *ch'an*, (from Sanskrit *dhyāna*) = meditation. The Buddhist sect originated in India, now popular in Japan.
2. Matthew 6:8. This same omniscience and omnipresence is wonderfully expressed in Psalm 139.
3. I Corinthians 3:18. For the life of me, I cannot see the congregation of cardinals fooling around.
4. Some of the data about Zen Buddhism was gleamed from A GLIMPSE OF NOTHINGNESS, by Janwillem van de Wetering [Simon & Shuster, New York] and THE RE-ENCHANTMENT OF EVERYDAY LIFE by Thomas Moore, [Harper-Collins, New York]

After countless years of searching, a monk approaches the country where Buddha lives. All he must do is to cross the wide, slow-moving river. As a boatman rows him across the monk casts a final glance on the world he leaves behind.

Then, on the lazy current, he sees a floating corpse.

The cadaver is carried closer. The monk screams as he recognizes his own body. All he has ever been, ever learned, ever owned, floats past him. It is the first moment of his liberation.

[A Chinese allegory]

24
GROUPS
(1)

When atoms combine into molecules, they initiate a process that grows in complexity. It is self-evident that the rise in quality necessitates an increase in constituent numbers. This law came into being at the time of the Big Bang, and it continues to be manifest today. At the other end of the spectrum we have a strange biblical saying *"Where two or three are gathered together in my name, there am I in the midst of them."*(2) Although both initiatives appear to advocate a tendency towards the formation of groups, in fact they are diametrically opposed. We may safely assume that whatever is conducive to the welfare of the material universe, is probably at odds with the subject matter of scriptural teaching. Even as, within dualistic reality, if we consider evil to be the opposite of good, then matter must represent the opposite of spirit.

Paradoxically, what is good for one may well be derogatory to the other. In time we realize that the opposites tend to work towards a common goal. But people steeped in material reality seldom perceive this.

The biblical quotation given above deals with the conversion of the subjective to the objective reality. A person who has an idea cannot share it, until he or she meets someone to share it with. If the two find agreement, become of like mind, [meet in my name or in my nature(3)] the idea becomes objective. That is why only two or three are needed.

Any larger number simply contributes spectators, or sheep that follow. They would not participate in the creative process, but merely take advantage of an accomplished fact. Thus, from the spiritual point of view, large groups are redundant. On the other hand, we need an endless stream of tiny groups of "two or three", for the creative process to continue. There is an infinite number of ideas extant in the limitless source (heaven), which we can bring out into the objective reality, for all to enjoy.

Finally, the group must be inevitably limited to two or three because the chances that more then this tiny number would agree on anything is too remote to contemplate. Due to the very fact that we, humans, are individuals with an infinite potential, we are, *per force*, extremely unlikely to agree on anything, let alone a new idea. History shows that it takes 20-25 years for any discovery to wend its way to general acceptance and/or application. Yet the ideas are as disparate as the creation itself. It is safe to assume that the divine Oneness manifests Itself through infinite diversity.

Although they will vehemently deny it, members of groups(4) are not yet fully developed individuals. The lower the life form the more it finds its expression within a group. We can hardly conceive of a single virus or bacterium. The difference between the lowest forms and the still nascent but relatively advanced units of consciousness is directly proportional to the awareness of their environment. A bacterium is aware only of the immediate environs controlling its survival. A mammal is aware of a much larger territory. Yet members of all groups recognize only the group's milieu as friendly environment. The world outside the group's control is the enemy.

Groups are thus the archetypes of the "us and them" syndrome.

From the spiritual point of view, groups of whatever species, organization or persuasion, are always expressions of a lower, less developed state of consciousness. Their dictum is "strength in numbers". They invariably place their own welfare above that of a competing organization. As long as groups exist, strife, conflict, exploitation, and wars will continue to flourish. All these may consolidate the "survival of the fittest", but do naught for our spiritual development. To gain and sustain power the constituents of a group often form oligarchic bands, such as governments, churches, armies, international conglomerates or trade unions. Due to the inherent weakness of component members, autocratic leaders often head such groups. As the group is their sole power-base, the bigwigs invariably place the welfare of the group before that of its component parts. In fact, the leaders will even sacrifice the lives of their own constituent members for the affluence, prestige or the survival of their organization. The governing systems are often called democratic—though usually only those elected officials stay in power that respond most judiciously to the popularity poles conducted at their bidding. Others are either expelled, or assassinated.

Quite apart of the above, the human consciousness continues to develop until it reaches a paradox. When it finally attains relative maturity, it is in position to impose its will on others with the greatest of ease. Yet, by now, in most cases, such a form of exploitation is abhorrent to it. Becoming an individual is synonymous with gaining enormous respect for the nascent potential of other life forms, including—and particularly—human. There follows a complete inversion of attitude. Rather than sacrificing others for the welfare of the group, they are prepared to sacrifice themselves to help even one other individual.

Though we affirm to the contrary, most of us resent others being different from ourselves. Our need for belonging, perhaps our hunger for Oneness, takes the form of a xenophobic fear of *non*-conformity. We think of individuals as odd, peculiar, perhaps abnormal. We seem to forget the adage about the mutual attraction of the opposites. Yet the price of freedom from these fears seems to lie in learning to find joy in diversity, in a profound respect for individuality, and in discovering that which we all have in common.

***
971029

FOOTNOTES

1. This essay has been reprinted, in part, in my book *VISUALIZATION / CREATING YOUR OWN UNIVERSE*, chapter on *Groups and Traditions* (about to be published as an ebook).
2. Matthew 18:20
3. Christ's nature is One. It does not suffer from the dualistic view of the material world. All is spirit or the manifestation thereof. It is this attitude, which was instrumental in Jesus' ability to perform miracles with such ease, though he too needed agreement from the "receiving" party
4. This subject has been discussed briefly in my essay *BEYOND RELIGION*, Volume I. [Inhousepress, Montreal 1997]

I asked a child, walking with a candle,
"From where comes that light?"
Instantly he blew it out.
"Tell me where it is gone—then I will tell you
where it came from."

Hasan of Basra

25
TEMPTATION

There are probably as many interpretations of the Lord's Prayer as there are people reciting it. My own thoughts on the subject are not intended to interpret the meaning but to update the symbology.

1. *Our Father –*

Our Father (God) is spirit. The scriptures state many times that unless we are born of the spirit we cannot enter the kingdom of heaven. Thus, unless we accept that we are also spirit, God is not our Father. Conversely, 'I and my father are one." This implies that I, as expressed by my Higher Self, am also spirit (even if sheathed in a physical body). Thus heaven is attainable for us.

2. *Which art in heaven –*

Heaven is a state of consciousness, of unqualified, unlimited potential realities. It can also be regarded as a Field of Infinite Possibilities. ["Whatsoever you ask... you shall receive"(1)]. Whatever we believe in—can and does happen. When we achieve the spiritual state of consciousness (Christ Consciousness), we can create any reality at will (though it might interfere with the objective realities of other, less advanced people). Once we accept *fully* that our true being is that of spirit, we lose all limitations.

3. *Hallowed be Thy name –*

This is best explained in the gospel of Thomas: "The kingdom is within you and it is without you", i.e. omnipresent. Hallowed simply means all-in-all, or whole.(2)

In the Bible, name always defines nature. We affirm that to us God is all-in-all, i.e. all is spirit, and thus a reality maintained by Divine Consciousness, of which we are an indivisible part. [All else is illusion].

4. *Thy kingdom come* –

We express our desire to bring about the conditions stated above. It is vital to remember that we can affect only *our own* state of consciousness. To attempt to affect others is equivalent to the use of black magic (see 2, above).

5. *Thy will be done on earth as it is in heaven* –

What is the Father's will—can be argued. Observing the world we can safely assume that the world is designed to give us joy, beauty and pleasure. Whoever does not believe that God and Good are synonyms, should not pray, as he will bring into his life whatever he believes in. To me, God symbolizes the omnipotent Consciousness, which is infinite in all perfections. By affirming this subjective truth, I bring It into my life, including my physical reality. In this clause, we also affirm our desire to become the "earthy" instruments of the divine will.

6. *Give us this day our daily bread* –

The *daily bread* symbolizes all that we need to partake in "joy, beauty and pleasure" of the created world, as well as our ability to bring these elements into our daily life. The term "this day" also places a limitation. We ask that we be given, or be instrumental in obtaining, only enough for our *daily* needs. We are not asking for an accumulation for the future. If we are not satisfied with living on a day-to-day basis, we should omit this clause from our prayer.(3)

7. *And forgive us our debts, as we forgive our debtors* –

No God ever "forgives" us our debts. The condition is stated clearly. As *we* forgive, so forgive us. We could almost say: "please help us to create opportunities through which *we* can settle our debts." All debts must always be paid. There are ample biblical parables to illustrate this point. What we are praying for here is detachment. We do not wish to be tied, hand and foot, to our past. Whatever happened, happened. We wish to be freed from our own "pangs of conscience". As we forgive our debtors, our consciousness is freed from anger, resentment, anxiety, etc.. We must remember that all prayers are always directed to the God within us, to our Higher Self, which is the only way we can communicate with the Infinite.

8. *And lead us not into temptation but deliver us from evil* –

This is a most vital clause to understand fully. The scriptures state that God is non-judgmental. "My Father judges no man".(4) The truth is staring us in the face. Let us look at our own lives. We each are the sum total of what we believe in. If we think (believe) we are poor, we are poor. If we think of ourselves as "intellectually challenged", we are. If our life is not filled with joy, it is because we have failed to fill it with joy. Remember? "Whatsoever you ask..." There are *absolutely no limitations* which our Higher Consciousness cannot bring about if we believe in It hard enough. But if we have the *slightest* doubt, all is lost. The spiritual consciousness *does not respond to ambiguity*, i.e. we cannot serve two masters. This is aptly illustrated in the Christ's temptation on the mountain.(5)

What is even more critical to understand is that since the Field of Infinite Possibilities is non-judgmental, the "not-so-good" people have equal access in this realm.(6) To put it in extreme terms, Christ and Hitler had equal access to the "Father". Perhaps this is why Hitler was instrumental in some 30,000,000 people losing their lives. The power in heaven is not only accessible to all, but is unlimited. What limits its use is our ability to exploit it, not its potential.

This clause, therefore, expresses our desire that we do not abuse this power made available to us. Because while we receive whatever we ask for, when any doubt sets in, all is lost. And then we have to start paying our debts. *All* our debts. "Till heaven and earth pass, one jot or one tittle shall in no wise pass from the law..."(7). The Field (heaven) responds to that which is "in our hearts", our subconscious, on an automatic basis. What we must learn is to bring about conditions through a conscious process. We must learn to gain access to heaven *consciously*. But when we do, we'd better watch out what we ask for. As we all know, absolute power corrupts absolutely.

***

971030

FOOTNOTES

1. Matthew 21:22 The condition, of course, is "believing".
2. from holy (from *halig* meaning holy), from (Germanic *hailagaz*) *hailaz* meaning WHOLE.
3. To emphasize the point: "Give us this day enough for a week", or "...this year enough for retirement" is not part of the deal. Spiritual life is always ONLY in the present.
4. John 5:22.
5. Matthew chapter 4.
6. Look up, again, essay #10, SPIRIT (The Ba Sotho of Transvaal)
7. Matthew 5:18, Luke 16:17.

*Whatever is received,
is received according to the nature of the recipient.*

Thomas Aquinas

26
LIMITATIONS

The purpose behind all great philosophies(1), or even incipient religions, is to help man out of his self-imposed limitations. It is self-evident that all things consisting of matter have their own characteristics, and are subject to indomitable laws. From subatomic particles all the way to complex biological organisms, their very nature defines their behavior pattern and thus their limitations. Even beyond particle physics, energy fields follow their predestined, invariably limited, modes of behavior. With this in mind, we must decide whether or not we are matter, or, more precisely, whether we identify exclusively with that which is the container of our consciousness. This consciousness, or self-awareness, is that which manifests itself within (or about) our body at (or about) the time of our birth. When it leaves, no biological entity remains alive.

Most people accept and identify with the duality of their nature, i.e. with body and soul. While they concede being hosts to a nondescript, non-identifiable, perhaps spiritual entity, which (they hope?) will assure their survival in the ever-after, on a day-to-day basis they are very much "physical" men and women endowed with senses, emotions and a mind. "I'm only human" is their unshakeable dictum. On Sundays, for an hour or so, these same people became temporary embodiments of souls, though even then they feel the need to beg, implore and beseech some external, equally nondescript, non-identifiable, probably spiritual entity for favors, which would free them, at least temporarily, from their limitations.

This accounts for most people I know.

The great Masters regard the nature of our being differently.

While conceding that their physical body does have limitations, they do not identify with their material embodiment to the same degree as most of us do. They do not accept, for instance, that we are essentially mortal animals, albeit (in some respects) superior to the rest of nature. The scientists take up this cry and, possibly leaning on the book of Genesis(2), assure us that we, humans, due to our superior power of reasoning, are definitely superior to all others species—a sort of "faunish" (or just faunal) *uber alles*.(3) Descartes propped up their claim with his famous: *Cogito, ergo sum*. Presumably, the moment Monsieur Descartes stopped thinking—he was no more. The great Masters, on the other hand, proposed that what differentiates us from one another (or from the animal kingdom) is not our intellect but our *state of consciousness*. The mystics, for the want of a better word, call the entity embodying this state—soul.

While this realization takes us a step further, we are only halfway there.

If we learn to identify principally with our state of consciousness, in other words, if we decide that it is not the body which determines our being (not to mention well-being), we certainly get rid of most of the limitations, which have been instilled in us by our dear parents, teachers, and representatives of various religions. Why religions? Because the inherent need of truth, which gnaws at our guts, makes us vulnerable to the preaching of all who *claim* to have the knowledge and ability to sate our inner hunger.

Alas, they seldom do.

While diminishing some of our belief in limitations by affirming the existence of an immaterial entity referred to as soul, they relegate such to a secondary position, by emphasizing the need for protecting our physical well-being, and to assure our future by atoning for our past. This way they place us firmly in the thongs of time, in the chains of temporal existence.

The Masters, and only the great Masters, dismissed such limitations.

Krishna, Buddha or Jesus affirmed their being outside all temporal constrains. While recognizing their material environment, they observed that while being in this world they were not *of* this world. It is rather like saying that while we may visit a country on holidays, we do not actually reside there. Visiting Mexico does not make us Mexicans. Conversely, a Mexican visiting Canada does not automatically become Canadian. Visiting the earth does not make us earthling. We remain, they say, souls—spiritual beings, regardless what cloth or body we wear. Our clothing/body is discardable, exchangeable, of relatively little importance. As souls, they do not recognize any limitations. Accepting that the body does place certain constrains on their freedom *while in it*, they recognize these as strictly temporary inconveniences.

Although, I venture to suggest, that while those Masters are incomparably superior to us, they always regarded the environment of their sojourn with the greatest respect. They did not break the natural laws, as we wouldn't when visiting a foreign country. They even treated the bodies they inhabited temporarily (don't we all?) with the respect allotted to a host who granted them an opportunity to learn, to observe, to experience. In this sense they accepted the limitations of their physical hosts. They did not accept, however, that they had been an intrinsic part of nature. In fact, they taught us how not to identify with the physical world. How to rise above it. They knew that once we become aware of *our* spiritual potential, we shall shed the dichotomy that has been imprinted on our minds. All limitations are the result of a *false* perception of our inherent duality. Rather like those of an actor assuming the limitations of the character he or she is portraying on the stage. When we realize this, we shall no longer be body and soul—but soul only.

We become One.

We must remember that there is absolutely nothing wrong with becoming deeply involved with the physical world. We can regard it as a most wonderful movie, a superb masterpiece, which a human body most assuredly is. We can become enamoured with making new, even better films. Cinematography can be such fun. But we should never, *never* forget that each film, no matter how brilliant, enchanting, on occasion tragic, melodramatic or comedic, is but a transient, ephemeral instant of our eternity. And when the film is over we shall leave the movies theatre and return to the *real* world. To our true home.

***

971102

FOOTNOTES

1. I use the term generically, i.e. from Greek *philos* meaning loving, and *sophos* meaning wise.
2. Genesis 1:28
3. German for "above others". W.F. Nietzche expanded this perverse concept with his ego-oriented notion of the *Uber mensch*—the superman.

Before garden vine or grape were in the world
Our soul was drunken with immortal wine.

Jalal-ud-Din Rumi

27
HEAVEN

Most people I know regard heaven as a sort of happy retirement camp. They picture themselves sitting outside their expensive condominiums, around their tepid pools, basking in the penumbra of the Royal palms; forever sipping their tall, cool Bloody-Marys, Manhattans or Martinis, and never being in danger of developing cirrhosis of the liver.(1)

Perhaps this heavenly indulgence will finally give due credit to the contention that liver is the seat of emotions and desire. Furthermore, in this heaven everyone will be very important. Since we shall all be clad in equally flowing robes (swimming trunks and costumes), no one will be able to tell how we made our living in the down-under. In fact, we shall all look pretty much alike. Regardless how we gorge ourselves, we shall display divine figures, full heads of hair, and equally as divine suntans. Skin cancer shall be abolished, as will all other diseases. They (nobody) will be able to tell if we came from Europe, the USA or Australia. There will be no Afro-Americans, Euro-Canadians, Sino-Europeans or Euro-Australians. English will be the spoken language, although some will speak Spanish and a few French (rather badly). It will be just like home. Retirement home. We shall all enjoy getting bored together. In style.

Others imagine heaven quite differently.

Some think that if they blow themselves to kingdom come while murdering some innocent people who disagree with their demands, they will take the elevator directly to paradise where they will be instantly surrounded by forty beautiful concubines, or women, or wives. I have a slight problem with this image of the ever-after, but that's probably because I enjoy, right now, quite enough problems with just one, single concubine, aah... woman, aah... wife. Actually she is whatever she chooses to be. I recall Shakespeare's prognosis: I *know I am too mean to be your queen, and yet too good to be your concubine.* Perhaps in heaven she can be all three. I'll just do my best to enjoy them all.

Then there are those who'd rather recline on a puffed-up, fluffy clouds, surrounded by ever-smiling, perhaps also forty, angels strumming their golden harps. I strongly suspect the angels would be attired in Mozartesque regalia, and be conducted by the immaculately tailed, fiddling Tarzan, known to the aficionados as André Rieu. They would play on and on and on. Forever and ever.(2)
Brrrrr....!
Given forty harpists (with or without André) versus forty beautiful concubines.... We all sleep with our choices.

***

And then we have the serious guys (and dolls).
They (we) will spend their (our) eternity at the feet of their (our) chosen deity (catalogue available at the gate), basking in His (Her) glory, rejoicing with the (above mentioned) angels. They (we) will be peeking down, way down, (with just the most innocuous of smirks) at the poor saps who still didn't even make it to the antechamber of the heavenly palace. Here we shall luxuriate in lavish and eternal peace, serenity, and peace. And serenity. Our joy will in no way be tempered by our knowledge (we shall be fairly omniscient) that our aunt and uncle, possibly also that second cousin (she was a bitch), are frying dead (though seemingly alive) on the sharp prongs of the glowing spits wielded by the long-tailed and horned (if not horny) devils.
Anyone for Florida?

For reasons of my own, I refuse to list the possible alternatives of hells (Gehenna, Hades, the Valley of Hinnom, Tartarus, are just some of the attractive-if-unseen locations) of which we also have a ready supply. The most prominent and popular of them all is the do-it-yourself hell. Surprisingly, some of these locations do *not* sound as bad as having to put up with forty wives, day in and day out (alternatively night in, night out) or, alternatively, to put it mildly—to getting bored stiff.

***

Is there a heaven?

That rather depends on the definition. If the question suggests that there is a place we *go* to, after we're dead and buried... I doubt it. I am deeply convinced that heaven is for the living, not for the dead. According to my reference book (the Bible), heaven is a state of consciousness. It is that, the awareness of which, we develop, over the years, perhaps over countless reincarnations. This same reference assures us that God resides in this elusive state, and since God is in heaven and heaven is within us...

A wondrous proposition.

To me, heaven is a state of consciousness, in which I shall forever have the opportunity to learn, to improve, to reach out further and further, without ever being in danger of reaching the end. It is an inexhaustible source that continues to supply the allurements and the challenges for my journey. It is a destination yet also a beacon in the endless ocean. It is infinite. I find infinity the most fascinating of concepts. For me it embodies eternity, unbounded intelligence or knowledge, eternal pursuit of the elusive; it means forever being beckoned, tempted, fascinated, and enchanted. For me heaven is also a condition in which I can share my joy with others; share my findings, discoveries, conquests. Forever. That's a really long time.

And my heaven embodies one other attribute. It is a state of consciousness wherein the greatest power is the power of love. In fact, there is none other.

***

971103

FOOTNOTES

1. Some people seem unaware that all drinks in heaven are tall and cool, in stark contrast to the hot and... in the other place.
2. For the uninitiated, André is a European import that, surrounded by crinolined ladies enthralls elderly ladies with his violin.

Surely for the god-fearing awaits a place of security,
gardens and vineyards
and maidens with swelling breasts, like of age,
and a cup overflowing.

LXXVIII
THE TIDING
[Arberry A.J. *THE KORAN INTERPRETED*,
Simon and Shuster, Touchstone, New York 1986].

28
DREAMING
OR
DOING NOTHING

I had a dream.
I dreamt that I might do what would be of greatest good to the greatest number. Many of us harbor such a dream, at one time or another. In the meantime we wait. One day, we say: when we're ready. When I am mature enough. When I've mastered the techniques. When I have something to say. You just wait. You'll see...

In the meantime, we do nothing—about the dream, I mean.

At first, we are not fully conscious of our dream. We dream at night, eyes closed, our metabolism slowed down, our brain drifting into alpha rhythm. There are also other types of dreaming. There is the type that churns for years and years at the very edge of our awareness, perhaps hovering in the no-man's land between our subliminal and waken reality. The important thing is to continue dreaming. When it finally comes to the forefront of our consciousness, it becomes incredibly vivid. All else, all other interests seem to wither, fall off. They do not disappear; they just fade into the domain of the not-so-important. That which once held topmost priority in our waken hours, now drifts into oblivion. Fragments of memory remain, rather like echoes of a thunderstorm, which is hardly heard, but still seen from a considerable distance. The memory of the lightening and the rumble is still frightening or enchanting, wistfully beautiful, but it's no longer of immediate concern. The dream is.

The greatest good to the greatest number of people...
How noble dreams can be!

Some people never discover their dream. They cross the journey of life at a half-hearted gait. They do what they feel they should, perform their duties—self imposed or delegated by other not-quite-awake pilgrims. Their lives are pleasant enough. They are neither miserable, nor really happy. They are the "I'm doing what I have to... to survive" type of people. They belong to the "I'm *only* human" group. They are the resigned-to-their-fate people. Abject humility.

They are the zombies. The living dead.

Are we?

We often do not discover our dream for many years. On some occasions we think we found it. We grasp it by the tail, swing it around and... let go. It was the wrong dream. I nearly became a concert violinist, an operatic singer, and a great architect. Nearly. I thought my heart was in every one of them. It was. There were also a dozen lesser rainbows, not quite making it to the starting gate. Each time I thought I threw everything I had into the dream. Perhaps I did. Hadn't there been some excuses? Good, very good reasons why other things became, at one time or another, more important? Or was that only after the spontaneity of the dream faded. I don't remember.

Perhaps... it doesn't matter.

The dream remained—elusive. Evasive, intangible, fleeting, imponderable, mysterious, insubstantial. Many of us seem to share this problem. The difficulty is in attempting to define that which is ineffable. We continue to struggle, to try too hard. We build our life on hope of achieving immortality even if in a tiny, minute area of our endeavor. A painter wants just a little fame. A sculptor just a little recognition. A writer, to be published, to see his name in print. The success is always in the future, in the realm over which we have relatively little control. Ah, but my dream is so noble...

So noble for whom?

Is advancing the longevity of human race the most noble of causes? Discovering a cure for cancer—enabling people to continue fumigating their lungs with nicotine and tar—is that noble enough? How about curing AIDS and thus empowering promiscuity, will that suffice? Or will exposing my creative urges in a public forum make me a better man? Will my soul rejoice as I take a deep bow at the book signing, a wine-gurgling *vernissage*?

So much to do, so little time.

The greatest good for the greatest number...

In whose opinion?

Am I a man dreaming I flew like a butterfly? Or am I a butterfly dreaming I walked like a man...

Waiting for a dream to manifest itself is a dream of folly. No matter how noble the dream, how great the aspirations. Great artists, writers, even saviors—are born, never made. There is no difference between a dream and reality. There is only a mode of being. Not doing, not striving, but being. I *am* a painter. I *am* a sculptor. I *am* a writer. I am a father, mother, clerk, teacher, priest, professional sportsman. *I am the best I can be*. The rest simply doesn't matter. My state of being needn't lead anywhere. It needn't even have tangible results. But I must be the very best I can be. That which I am today is a thousand times better than a thousand dreams, which might remain unfulfilled.

I remember telling my young friend how to be, or to act––by doing nothing. About *wu wei* the concept of "taking no action".(1) She threw up her arms in exasperation: "You might as well give up!" was her immediate reaction, "What's the point of trying!?" None, I replied. Stop trying, just be. Just be the best you can...

But... but...

... the best that you can be. Never mind the results.

I am a butterfly dreaming I'm a man.

Non-doing does not mean doing nothing. It simply means avoiding the deliberate, the thought out, rather than putting one's faith in the spontaneous. It means living your dreams rather than dreaming about them. (Perhaps you too are a butterfly?) It means responding to your inner voice, the unconscious—if you like. Perhaps I had once been a concert violinist—I have played concertos; an operatic singer—I sang most glorious basso arias, a "great" architect—as good I could have been, at the time. Perhaps had I been better, the buildings would have never been built. Perhaps I didn't dream my dreams, perhaps I lived them.

"The greatest good to the greatest number," now sounds rather presumptuous. Almost pompous. Such delusions may indeed be relegated to the field of dreams, providing they are first salted with a pinch of humility. We don't know what the future holds for us. We do know that today we, every one of us, can and must respond to our inner calling. And only to that calling. Other than that, we must commit ourselves to do absolutely nothing.

Perhaps life is but a glorious dream.

***

971122

FOOTNOTE

1. The Chinese expression: Wu *wei er wu pu wei*, literally: "taking no action, there is no not acting" is attributed to Lao Tsu, though, according to D.C. Lau, the expression does not in fact occur in the excavated texts at all. For further reading see: *LAO TSU, TAO TE CHING*, Translation of the Ma Wang Tui Manuscripts by D.C. Lau [Everyman's library, Alfred A. Knopf, Inc. Publ.1994] (*Introduction* pg. xxvii)

29
PETER

It never ceases to amaze me how the hunger for power can change people who would otherwise remain decent members of the human family. No matter how well meaning, how well intentioned, a mere whiff of power seems to cloud our eyes and ears, close our minds to elementary logic, even to common sense with which, surely, we are all inherently endowed. Forcing a Triple Crown on Peter's brow, is a case in point.

Some considerable time ago, a man of quite unprecedented talents spent some years looking for a practical example to embody his teaching. Heretofore, he lacked a single man or woman, a single disciple on whom he could hang his mantle. Not the mantle of power, of authority, but simply to illustrate, to *interpret*, what his teaching was all about. Finally his search came to an end. The teacher was Jesus, the disciple—Peter. The same Peter who thrice denied any knowledge of Jesus. The same Peter whose faith faltered when he attempted to walk on water. But also the Peter who said: Thou art the Christ, the Son of the living God. And since Peter could only have known this by listening to his inner voice, Jesus replied: Thou art Peter, and upon this rock I shall build my church.

Who was this Peter?

I would bet that if Peter had been an intellectual giant, a man of uncommon organizational abilities, he would not have been selected. You don't need these traits to be a fisherman. What a fisherman needs is a good doze of faith that when he casts his nets into the dark waters, he will catch something; on occasion, he must be stubborn yet flexible. He must always believe that he will get back to the shore in one piece; that adverse winds will not smash his boat against the rocks. There must have been many occasions when Peter had little to rely on but his faith in the protection of the Almighty. We all seem to gravitate that way when all else fails. No one more so than a fisherman.

He was certainly no candidate to build a world religious organization. In any case, anyone who ever took the trouble to do some basic research knows that Paul founded the incipient ecclesiastic organization, not Peter. No one would dream of entrusting power to such a cowardly, floundering, even treacherous individual as Peter. The fact that Peter later made up for his moments of weakness in no way changes what he had been at the time. When referring to Peter as the rock, what Jesus was endeavoring to show his other disciples was that the whole development of the human psyche, human soul, is build on faith. That we must listen to our inner voice. No matter how weak, how inept, how cowardly we might feel, faith is the immovable rock, the indispensable component of progress. It is the single, unique motivating force pushing us forward. It is the force of life, of evolution.

Why?

Progress is invariably based on the movement from the known to the unknown. At the time when a new idea anchors itself tremulously in your mind, you and only you are aware of that idea. Let us not forget that *all* original ideas can come *only* from within. And so, of the billions of people populating this ball of dust, there are moments when you, and you alone, are the harbinger of the Good News. Nothing, absolutely nothing but faith is your ally at this time. Without faith this new idea will never see the light of day. Faith and faith alone can motivate you to bring it out into the open, perhaps risking ridicule, opposition from people in power, perhaps danger to your life. The new is always risky. Faith sustains you. On faith we build our future. And Peter, in spite of all his foibles, had faith. Perhaps not the strongest, but he was prepared to act on it, if only with words.

"Thou art nobody, but show me a single act of faith and I shall build an awareness, an assembly of thoughts, a church, upon it. And no thoughts of limitation shall prevail against it. For faith is the key to the wondrous field of Infinite Possibilities"

What is a church?

The word is a translation from Greek *ekklesia* meaning "that which is called out." The idea is that from the effulgence of thoughts that churn in our cluttered, overworked minds, some thoughts, some ideas are called out for the sole purpose of serving God. These thoughts are not only the called, they are the called *out*. The chosen. We all know the expression "many are called but few are chosen". Well, so it is with a church. From the many that are called, some are called out. They are selected, set aside, for a specific purpose. Those that are set aside, the chosen ones, are the church.

We must never forget that no group, religious or any other, had been created unto the image of God. Only an individual can aspire to this title. Groups, no matter how well meaning, no matter how illustrious titles they bestow upon themselves, are all transient, inferior to a single I AM. The soul only, and only the soul is destined to be immortal. When you build your church, you build your state of consciousness. *Your* consciousness. No one can do it for you. No group, no religious body, no organization.

There is but one church that matters. And that, in the words of King David, is the secret place of the most High. It is a good place to be. The place of the chosen.

***

971211

*Fishes, asking what water was,
went to a wise fish.
He told them that it was all around them,
yet they still thought that they were thirsty.*

Nasafi
Shah, Idries THE SUFIS
[Doubleday & Co., Inc. New York, 1964, pg. 356.]

30
THE GREATEST CRIME

On **Sunday, December 7, 1997** a strange account appeared in the Montreal Gazette. In an interview with Rev. Bill Phipps, the moderator of the United Church of Canada, a question was raised: "Was Jesus God?" It transpired that the titular head of a Christian denomination did not think so. He did not think that Jesus was God. I can see the shock-waves spreading across Christianity like the ripples from an enormous meteorite striking an ocean of believers. The ripples that might well change our Christian climate for a long time to come. Perhaps forever.

Does it matter?

In my essay *The Message and the Messenger*(1), I stressed the importance of not confusing the one with the other. The greatest crime is to deify the messenger while ignoring his message. God, a universally accepted symbol of infinity, cannot be assumed to find Its total expression through that which is finite. No matter how great, how wonderful the messenger. There are those who might say that Mozart is music, that Einstein is astrophysics, that Renoir is Impressionism. But these are terms of affection, having their origin in our emotions, springing from our hearts. So be it. There are moments when Jesus denotes an embodiment of divinity. There are moments when Buddha assumes this function. Sometimes I see God in the beauty of a flower, or hear Him in the voice of a nightingale, or even in the music of Mozart.

But God is not sometimes. God is always. And God cannot be chopped up, decimated, quantified. To me God is All in All. It is That which finds Its expression through Its creation. But He, IT, is also all That which has not been expressed as yet, perhaps never will be. Though never is such a long time....

Was Jesus God?
I am reminded of the Christ's question: "Why callest thou me good? There is none good but one, that is God..."(2). Doesn't sound like God talking. "And call no man your father upon the earth: for one is your Father, which is in heaven"(3). We are all created in the image of that which is perfect, in the image of our Father. Image. All of us. What we do with this image later... but that's quite another story.

"The servant is not greater than his lord; neither he that is sent greater than he that sent him"(5). Neither greater nor equal. Nor is the Messenger greater than the Message.

"I can do nothing on my own...."

Our identification with the object of our contemplation is limited by our mind. The Spirit is above the mind. We regard It as That which has no limitations. For as long as we are imprisoned in our physical bodies, we cannot reach out beyond them. Not completely. And even then, when we do free our spirit, we might, if we so desire, be able to merge with that which IS. Become integral with IT. To lose our personality is to merge into Buddha's Nothingness.(6) Not to become IT to the exclusion of all other. That would be to limit That (I am That I am) which is beyond limitations.

I have never met a Christian who did justice to the teaching of Christ. [Perhaps I've been unlucky]. And I've never heard one to affirm the nature of his or her own being using the words: I and my Father are one. *Not* I am my Father. A drop in an ocean is one with the water therein. It is not the ocean itself. Whether some Christians recognize Jesus as their God is of no consequence. The question is: have they heard his message? Because those who dismiss Jesus as a prophet might be excused from following his teachings, but those who deem him God and still ignore him, commit the greatest of crimes.

Since the purpose of prayer is to become one with the object of one's contemplation, Jesus became one with that which he taught. The Way. The Method. The System. Surely his purpose was to show us how to proceed, how to realize life in its fullness. Not by our own power, but by hooking up onto the current of Infinite Potential. "The Son can do nothing of himself,"(7) he repeated. A god who can do nothing of himself? We all are but channels for the creative spirit. All of us. Some more perfect than others. And what have the Christians done to their acclaimed leader? Against all his statements, lessons, instructions, admonishments, they... deified him. It must have felt good to have one's feet washed, vicariously, by God!(8)

The greatest of all crimes...

By creating an insurmountable barrier of divinity between us and the Christ, the Christian churches have shut the gates of heaven in our faces. Surely, no man can do what the Christ has done. After all, was he not God? Ask any Christian!

Did Jesus ever lay claim to divinity? Has he even averred his own, let alone divine, power? *The son can do nothing of himself....* Yet whoever believes in the Way, in the Method: greater *works than these shall he do.*(9) Greater than God?

No man is greater than his master.

The greatest of all crimes was perpetrated by the collusion of the so-called Christian churches in order to usurp power in the name of the man who showed us consummate humility. A million churches, a thousand Vaticans, an army of Popes resplendent in their snowy attire amid a sea of crimson robes, could never do justice to the message which Jesus showed us. A billion candles burning to his glory would not cast a wisp of a shadow compared to a single ray of the light that he shone upon us.

Was Jesus God? Not according to his own testimony. Was he the Son of God? I'll let the psalmist answer: "Ye are

gods; and all of you are children of the most High. But ye shall die like man, and fall like one of the princes."(10)
Even the greatest of princes.

***
971212

FOOTNOTES

1. BEYOND RELIGION, VOLUME I. [Inhousepress, Montreal 1997, Smashwords Edition 2010]
2. Matthew 19:17
3. Matthew 23:9
4. John 13:16
5. Personality is a characteristic of the ego, individuality of the soul. It is my contention that the loss of personality does not entail loss of identity. We retain an individual awareness, which is an inherent, indestructible attribute of Soul.
6. John 5:19 et al.
7. John 13:5...
8. John 14:12
9. John 14:15
10. Psalm 82: 6-7, compare John 10:34

A lamp am I to you that perceive me
A mirror am I to you that know me

Apocryphal Acts of John

31
WHAT IS CÆSAR'S

"Render unto Cæsar the things that are Cæsar's..." (1)

Who or what is this Cæsar to whom we are to hold such an allegiance?

Briefly, Caesar is the result. God is the cause. You can choose to align yourself with either. Until we accept this seemingly innocuous division, we are at a loss to understand biblical admonitions. There is a presumed paradox, though it dissolves itself the moment we accept the admonitions seriously.

I continue to meet people who insist that the Bible provides historical, geographical or perhaps even anthropological information. While such a stance may have some peripheral substance, it is rather like saying that in order to delve into the history of the Roman Empire, we should study Shakespeare's Julius Cæsar. We can. We might actually learn something about early Rome, as we might learn something about the Danish Royal House by studying Hamlet. But surely, no scholar, not even an aspiring beginner, would seriously suggest that Shakespearean plays should be studied (exclusively or even mostly) for their historical content! Yet some people take the books of Moses, the various Prophets, the New Testament, and proceed to treat them as an archaeological dig. They end up with indisputable data attesting to the human race having its origin with Adam in 4004 B.C.. While this "first man" reputedly lasted 175 years (probably due to lack of mortal enemies), a mere 126 years after his death, Noah, ostensibly due to acute shortage of good hired help in his ark construction business, had to increase his life-span to just fifty short of a millennium.(2) Yet in all this time, in spite of such shortage of good men, he had... only three sons! By contrast, his later successor, Solomon, during his mere 58-year life-span, collected 700 wives plus 300 concubines. Assuming he started doing them justice at say 16, then, on average, with just half the females having access to their lord and master once-a-month (in rotation), that's 16 women per night, every night, and a *ménage à dix-sept* now and again, for 42 years straight.(3)

Tiring.

The fundamentalists will also prove that the sun (and the moon) periodically stood still(4) in its whirling around the earth, though regrettably too late to take advantage of the 22.5 feet of water(5) which would have kept the whole earth cool on such occasions. The same scholars will also quote whole passages from the Bible to prove that a crowds of people merrily crossed some 200 kilometers of soggy, muggy, boggy, bottom of the Red sea, while a few miles north they could have reached the desert with clean sandals. Can you imagine? With a bunch of children, elderly and whatever equipment they could scrounge from the Egyptians (not to mention being heavily laden with piles of gold for the production of idols), they could have moved at, say, 30 kilometers a day. It would have taken them seven days of sea-bottom-walking (camping, sleeping, eating, hunting, etc.?), while the waters and the Pharaoh's hordes in hot pursuit, all held their collective breath! Thereafter, the poor sods kept walking in circles for forty years, in the middle of a most inhospitable desert, with nothing to show for it but mighty sore feet. Surely if Moses and his successors wanted to write history instead of a record of spiritual development, they could have done much better than this. The Bible is full of such anthropological tidbits for those who take them literally. And there are many that do—some of whom I count among my friends. Somehow, perhaps due to some insidious conditioning, they refuse to accept that the Bible had been written for the edification of the soul, not of the body. For the timeless, not the transient. For the real, not the illusory.

Charles Fillmore, the renowned pioneer in metaphysical thought, compares those seeking historical information in the Bible to the Pharisees: "The Pharisees of Jesus' time were condemned by Him for teaching the letter of the Scriptures and neglecting the spirit. The same charge can be brought today against those who study the Bible as history rather than as parable and idealistic illustration of the spiritual unfoldment of man."(6)

So why did Moses and other inspired teachers employ symbolic vernacular to record their *spiritual* insights? Because "this is the only possible way in which knowledge could be given to people in all ages, in different part of the world, and of different degrees of spiritual development."(7) The very fact that many people still question this very premise attests to the veracity of Emmet Fox's statement.

So what of Cæsar?

In the days Jesus walked the earth, Cæsar symbolized all that was material, physical or carnal—just as Egyptians did to Moses. There is absolutely nothing wrong with the material, physical or carnal world, nothing at all. In fact, nothing illustrates the indescribable beauty and creative potential of the Spirit better than that which has already been created. All the animals, flowers, trees, rivers and mountains, the stars, galaxies... even some people, are all a direct result of the munificent generosity and inconceivable diversity of the Creative Life Force. How could we not admire such beauty? And all of it is Cæsar's. All are the results. And what the Great Masters endeavored to teach us was how to procure such results. In fact, they gave us shortcuts to success. To the domain of Cæsar. And all that Cæsar expects in exchange is a little maintenance. A little TLC. The only problem is that in spite of our efforts, all things that are Cæsar's are subject to the inexorable laws, which cause all that has been created of matter to be transient, to hover on the brink of extinction, to persist in a state of decay.

What the great Teachers taught us was how *not* to die. How *not* to get attached to that which is ephemeral. They taught us how to live.

No matter how beautiful our body, or character, or even our mind and personality, they are all transient. *We* don't have to be. We don't have to identify with decay, anguish, death. We can be immortal. We can become part of the Eternal Cause, self perpetuating, self rejuvenating, self replenishing expressions of that which IS. No symbols are necessary to state this truth today.

But then? In the days of yore?

How would a kindly if simple, warm-hearted if illiterate, shepherd or merchant, or his wife or daughter, understand that the distance between the various atoms comprising his or her physical body is so great that we all are essentially... nothing? Just nothing. Void. Empty space.(8) For that matter, how many people accept it today? How many people can visualize the world as a matrix of thoughts interlocking innumerable ideas into transient states of objective existence, into that which we call the observable, material or manifested universe? And yet, this is the true nature of reality in which we find our being. We are not the universe; the universe is our composite shadow, even as our physical bodies are precise shadows of our individual minds; and minds are the creative instruments of our souls. Is it any wonder that Moses or Jesus have chosen to use allegories, parables and symbols to explain these concepts?

Is it?

So let us give Cæsar his due.

He and his world is the product of the Creative Life Force. We, you and I, have created Cæsar. We, individualizations of the One Cause, are his mother and father. We brought together some elements, stirred them with our emotions, and shaped them with our thoughts. We sustained them, a while, with the breath of Life. Let us hope, when we vacate the shells of our making, someone will look upon our ashes and say, as Mark Antony had once said of Cæsar:

> *His life was gentle, and the elements*
> *So mix'd in him that Nature might stand up*
> *And say to all the world*
> *'This was a man!'*
> (9)

***

971216

FOOTNOTES

1. ...and unto God the things that are God's. Matthew 22:21
2. In the Bible his life span is given as 951 years (2949 - 1998 BC). It may be of interest that he was also known as Xisurthrus (to the Babylonians), Yao or Fo-Hi (Chinese), and as Prometheus, Deucalion, Atlas, Theuth, Inachus, Osiris, Dagon etc, in other cultures.
3. 1000 (wives & concubines) ÷ 2 = 500 x 12 (months) = 6000 ÷ 365 days = 16.4 women per night
4. Habakkuk 3:11, Joshua 10:12-13.
5. Genesis 8:20: 5 cubits = 22.5 feet (6.86 meters). N.B.: and yet... "the *mountains* were covered." ibid. Perhaps this is the origin of the (almost) Flat Earth (concept) Society.
6. Phillmore, Charles MYSTERIES OF GENESIS, *Foreword*, [Unity School of Christianity, Unity Village. Mo. 64063]
7. Fox, Emmet ALTER YOUR LIFE [Harper & Row Publishers, New York.]
8. It has been proposed that the distance between various atoms in our bodies is, in proportion, as the distance between the earth and the sun.
9. Shakespeare, William JULIUS CAESAR

*We are floating in a medium of vast extent,
always drifting uncertainly,
blown to and fro;
We burn with desire to find a firm footing,
an ultimate, lasting base
on which to build a tower rising up to infinity,
but our whole foundation cracks and the earth opens..."*

                         Virginia Woolf
                            [Pensés]

32
AQUARIUS & URANUS

In my essay: *Cycles*(1) we discussed the general principles governing the Zodiac, or more accurately, the way that Zodiac controls or governs us. This principle of control is often misunderstood. In the physical universe everything influences everything else. This interrelationship brings about conditions, which result in laws such as those expressed in the Theory of Relativity, Quantum Mechanics, as well as laws regulating the biological and zoological interrelationships. In the objective reality of time and space, all is relative yet subject to, what the Bible calls, the Law.(2) It is neither restrictive nor vindictive, but merely a statement that this is how the world works.(3) These various laws can be summed up in, and extended into, a single law of Cause and Effect, or what the Eastern mystics call the Law of Karma.

It is not so in the domain of Spirit. When we make a conscious jump, a quantum leap from the objective to the subjective reality, we free ourselves from any and all constrains. We are no longer subject to the laws of the universe. We enter a realm, rather like the heart of a Black Hole, wherein the laws of physics no longer hold sway.

This is the Truth that sets us free.

In order to achieve this freedom, we go through a series of lessons that bring us closer to this enigmatic liberation. The various signs of the Zodiac, each taking about 2150 years, express these lessons. Of the twelve sings, the Bible takes us back only two segments, to the sign called Aries, the Ram. A few centuries into the age of Aries, after the period of adjustment, the first great teacher called Abraham promulgated the first Good News. In Hebrew, his name means, "father of a multitude", which has been promptly misunderstood to mean the "father of the Jewish nation". In fact, the "multitude" refers to the stream of (creative) thoughts, which invade our minds in a prolific volume and intensity. When Abraham became aware of this condition (the stream of thoughts), he changed his name to Abram, meaning, "father of height". "Height", in the Bible, invariably symbolizes a *raised* state of consciousness. During the age of Ram, our lessons have been directed towards bringing our thoughts under control. In the Bible, the sheep (rams) symbolize our thoughts, the shepherds—all who controlled them. A Good Shepherd is he who gained total control over his thought-stream.

Some two millennia later, the human race entered the next sign of the Zodiac, called Pisces, or the Fishes. The new great teacher was, of course, Jesus of Nazareth. Pisces or Fishes always symbolized wisdom. From the Persian kings of yesteryear to the popes and bishops of today, the patriarchal men like to wear a tiara, a hat in the shape of a fish's head, to symbolize the marriage of Knowledge (Intelligence) and Love. The synthesis of these ingredients results in Wisdom. And essentially this was the teaching of the Piscean age: to imbue our controlled thoughts with love.

Finally we have reached the Age of Aquarius.

If we have learned our previous two lessons well, then the New Age will bring us fantastic joy and indescribable rewards. If not... one day we shall get another chance.

Let us assume that we have acquired a reasonable control over our thoughts. Let us assume that we all know, therefore, that that which we think [in our hearts(4)] will inevitably manifest itself in our lives. In other words, whatever we truly believe in will become our reality. If we expect calamity, the chances are such will befall us. If our hearts are filled with expectations of prosperity, prosperity shall be ours. It is the Law. And for this very reason the second lesson (Pisces), the one in which we have learned Wisdom, is of such tremendous importance. Theoretically we could have moved directly from Aries to Aquarius. We have already acquired powers beyond comprehension. We could say to the mountain: remove thyself, and, if our faith or thought control were sufficient, it would.(5)

Nothing is impossible for us.(6)

Such power, without love, would be the most devastating power in the universe. It is to be hoped that no man learned the first without learning the second. The Karma resulting from the abuse of one's mind is called Black Magic, only today it can be used on a tremendous scale. It is not manifested in sporadic parlor tricks for the amusement of our friends, but in vast concentration camps, in holocausts of many nations, in bringing us to the very brink of a nuclear extinction. Unless love or wisdom prevails, we are lost. During the transitional period, a number of men have, and continue to abuse this power.(7) During the age Aquarius, most of us shall have the ability to wield power beyond our wildest dreams.

At the moment things appear to be looking up. The nuclear holocaust seems to be, at least temporarily, averted. The United Nations appears to be developing a global conscience. The powerful nations are beginning to share their riches with the poorer.

There is hope. There is always hope.

But...

There is one other problem to be considered. The problem of Uranus. He is, of course, yet another symbol. In Greek mythology, Uranus or *Ouranos*, was a god who personified heaven. Uranus confirms what Saint John the Divine affirmed in his Revelation when he wrote: I make all things new.(8) "Heaven" always does.

Regrettably, to make room for the new the old must be destroyed.

Most people, who accept the concept of periodic renewal, do not seem to understand that one cannot put new wine into old skins.(9) It simply cannot be done. Jesus explained why. Skins symbolize our states of consciousness, and those include our attachments, traditions, and old comfortable ways. And our ways include our day-to-day life as well as our organizations, international relations, and... religions. Our whole world-view. "Behold, I make all things new." ALL of them. This seems to be the hardest thing for us to accept.

Fortunately, the Law allows us a period of adjustment.

In the meantime, we ventured into the Aquarian Age: quietly, almost unannounced. Its precursors were the various Charters of Individual Rights. It showed its arrival more forcibly with the onset of Industrial Revolution. With the Technological Revolution it got into full swing. The symbol of the New Age is a man with a watering can. It symbolizes the empowerment of the individual. We shouldn't look for a single great teacher, but rather for scattered men and women, who already have and will continue to appear at the right time, in the right place, the world over. Another way of describing this process is the "Second Coming", only the "coming" will not be embodied in a single individual but will occur in people's hearts, their states of consciousness.

Aquarius is the age of the individual.

He who has learned the last two lessons, (even if at present the knowledge only churns at his or her subliminal level), has almost two thousand years to water his private garden. Two thousand years to demonstrate his understanding, to build a new state of consciousness. We have entered the age, in which every individual shall find the means to free himself from the oppression of any and all pressure groups. Groups are the old skins of the past age—gradually they will die out. But we shall not enter anarchy. We shall enter a new age of enlightenment wherein altruism

will no longer be regarded as a virtue, but as an exigent expression of self-preservation.
Good luck.

**
971217

FOOTNOTES

1. BEYOND RELIGION vol. 1. [Inhousepress, Montreal 1997, Smashwords Edition 2010].
2. In his book THE AMAZING LAWS OF COSMIC MIND POWER (Parker Publ. Co., N.Y.), Joseph Murphy D.D., D.R.S., Ph. D., LL. D., writes; "The scientific thinker substitutes the word "Law" for "Lord" in the Bible. This is the law of your subconscious mind, which magnifies whatever you deposit in it. It is an impersonal law of cause and effect."
3. Matthew 5:18 puts it this way: "Till heaven and earth pass, one jot or one tittle shall no wise pass from the law, till all be fulfilled."
4. i.e. that which is imbedded in our subconscious mind.
5. Matthew 17:20
6. ibid.
7. The preponderance of "suicide bombers", Wall Street scandals, African genocides, all provide ample example of this. (March 2009)
8. Revelation 21:5
9. Matthew 9:17, Mark 2:22, Luke 5:37;

*The more I observe and study things,
the more convinced I become that sorrow over separation
and death is perhaps the greatest delusion.
To realize that it is a delusion is to become free.
There is no death, no separation of the substance.*

Mohandask K. Gandhi
(1869 - 1948)

[Better known as Mahatma (great-soul) Gandhi. The quotation is an extract from a letter to Madeleine Slade, a British admiral's daughter who renounced her position to follow Gandhi]

33
I AM THAT I AM

Anyone who ever listened to a sermon in any Christian church knows full well that God is in heaven. The Catholics also find him hidden in the Holy Eucharist. Moses, born some 1571 years before Christ, did not have such an advantage. Having no churches or temples to attend, he found his God in the desert. Having met Him, privately, Moses asked what is His name. And God replied, I AM THAT I AM.

There is considerable evidence that Moses was a historical figure, and that he did author, *inter alia*, the second book of the Torah, the *Exodus*. It is in this book that he shared with us his momentous realization; the single phrase which should have changed the history of the world. Alas, no such luck. The tribes of his day, even as my friends of today, do not seem to recognize the import of his message. They prefer to treat his words as yet another mystery, yet another excuse, to ignore the reality. And if there are people who understand this simple phrase, they seem to refuse to accept it.

Most people I know, if they search for God at all, they continue to do so in churches, temples, synagogues. They can't search for God in heaven because the sacerdotal ranks refuse to tell them where heaven is. Moses was lucky. In his day there was hardly any clergy. None to speak of.

For some reason people find Moses' statement enigmatic. Would "I AM this very same I AM", or "I AM this I AM and there is no other", be any easier? Or perhaps "This I AM and that I AM are one-and-the-same"; would such an elaboration help? Why did the ancient Hebrew prefer to worship golden idols, even as today's Christians prefer gilt statues, icons, ossified relics in papal rings, tombs, or even the content of a tabernacle?

Is it that people like mysteries?

Yet... there are no mysteries.

Or, to be more precise, the only mysteries that exist are deep within our own hearts. Deep within our own minds. We create mysteries at the same rate at which the great teachers, prophets and saviors endeavor to dispel them.

Who shall I say has sent me, asked Moses? "...say unto the children of Israel, I AM hath sent me unto you."(1) And later: "Thou shall have no other gods before me."(2)

I AM THAT I AM. And no other gods.

No other gods, idols or objects of worship.

None.

The Bible reiterates Moses' statement many times, if in slightly different form. A number of Hebrew names attempt to grind into our awareness the very same truth. *Joel* means Jah is El. Jah, an abbreviation of Jehovah or YAHWEH, [the universal male and female principle] is El [the unifying principle within the human entity]. That is what the name means. The I AM and *that* I AM are one and the same.

Eliah, means El is Jah, exactly same as Joel only in reverse order. Later we meet *Eliah* (El is Jah) and *Eliel*, meaning El is El, or God is God, or I AM THAT I AM. And none other. Yet in spite of those tedious repetitions people refuse to understand that the only God they will ever encounter is El, the God within, the Higher Self. They cannot meet, face to face or otherwise the Jah, (the Yahweh or Jehovah) because the Jah is not a person, nor even a Being, but the Principle. Yet the qualitative essence expressed by the concept of Jehovah is exactly the same as that expressed by the concept of El. And all this has been stated many, many times in the Bible. We can ignore it, providing we do not call ourselves Christians. Why? Because when Jesus said, "I and my Father are one," he repeated the very same truth. "I who am born of Spirit, and the Spirit of which I am born, are one and the same." There is none other.

How could it be otherwise?

***

For some reason people suffer from a great need to exteriorize the divine. It is as if God manifested His presence in the whole universe, everywhere—except within them. Surely, if God, the Universal Creative Life Force, is omnipresent, then we cannot exclude Its presence from our own hearts. Sometimes it seems that many Christian churches encourage this dichotomy. For what reason? Perhaps in order to usurp the power flowing from assuming the role of an intermediary. To stand between El and Jehovah. Or between us and El. Don't they know that, in truth, we and El are one? That without El's presence we would "give up the ghost"? There is great danger that if people ever start reading the Bible, the churches will lose power over their minds. No church can enter a man's heart, yet that is where El resides. In all His glory.

El is the Principle personified. It is the I AM. God.

And when Moses turned 80, he reminded us about it over 3500 years ago. Had anyone listened?(3) Does anyone listen today?

For some reason Christians seem to imagine that since the adoption of the Julian calendar(4), all pre-Christian philosophies should be discarded or, at the very least, relegated to irrelevant historical *curiosa*. This in spite of Jesus' assurances that he had come not to "destroy the law, but to fulfil it"—presumably as we all should.(5) Yet even within the Roman Church there had been some brave enough (though admittedly unconventional) who did not succumb to this weakness. St. Augustine, one of Christendom greatest thinkers said: "That which is called the Christian religion existed among the ancients and never did not exist from the beginning of the human race."(6) Unfortunately it does not seem to be known at the Vatican.

What Moses told us was always known—to those who searched.

There is no mystery in these words. It is a statement of simple truth. Truth available to every man, woman and child who take the trouble to enter the secret chamber of their own heart. Some five-hundred years ago, Paracelsus, in his *Philosophia Occulta,* has this advise: "Let us depart from all ceremonies, conjurations, consecrations, etc., and all similar delusions, and put our heart, will and confidence solely upon the true rock... If we abandon selfishness the door will be opened for us, and that which is mysterious will be revealed."(7)

Perhaps Moses could have added: I AM, and I AM WAITING.

***

971231

FOOTNOTES

1. Exodus 3:14
2. ibid. 20:3
3. Born in 1571 B.C., Moses left Egypt at the age of 40 only to return there after spending some 40 years in Midian. Since he is said to have died at the age of 120 (in 1451 B.C.), in order to be able to wander some 40 years in the desert, he must have been about 80 when he lead his people out of Egypt. While there is considerable evidence that Moses was a historical figure, I would strongly discourage anyone from taking the chronological data literally. (If we were to do so, we would be forced to concede that Adam had been "created" in 4004 B.C.). [Data gleamed from ANALYTICAL CONCORDANCE TO THE BIBLE by Robert Young, LL.D.; WM.B. Eerdmans Publ. Co., Michigan 1980]
4. corrected by Pope Gregory XIII in 1582
5. Compare Matthew 5:17.
6. Saint Augustine (354-430), Doctor of the Church. [Epistolae Lib. I, xiii]. His autobiographical CONFESSIONS and his CITY OF GOD are still very popular.
7. Philippus Aureolus Paracelsus c.1493 - 1541, Swiss physician, alchemist and chemist. Also refer to my essay #15, *Mystery*, hereinbefor

34
MARRIAGE

We all seem to think that we are endowed with free will. This misconception is probably the last illusion that we shall be ultimately willing to let go. In the meantime, most of us will remain enslaved to our conditioning, traditions, customs and mores, and all the acquired knowledge that controls our tiny microcosms.

By contrast, people who truly aspire to free will not only do not recognize any external influences as dominant in their lives, but also tend to lean heavily on intuition. Furthermore, though it may sound paradoxical, it is only by giving up the *illusory* free will associated with our ego that we can attain true freedom. It is rather like dying in order to live, or choosing macrocosm over microcosm. What it really means is that the Whole must become more important than anyone of Its parts. We can only achieve this realization by asserting that our true Self is an indivisible part of the Whole. When adopting this world-view, we remain fully aware of the trappings and wiles of the material, or the fragmented reality, but we regard them from the perspective of an interested observer. What is more vital, we are no longer directly affected by them.

Those among us who choose to remain within the egocentric orientation are subject to entropy: a sort of physio-socio-energetic insipid communism.(1) Such people are concerned, principally, with their just portion of the manifested universe, preferably according to their needs, rather than efforts. Their gain must be someone else's loss. This world-view is, of course, in direct opposition to the teachings of the great Masters who endeavored to show man how to liberate himself from this tiresome and limiting attitude; how to become integral to the Cause rather than remain an insignificant effect. And finally, how to draw on the inexhaustible storehouse of Infinite Potential. Surely, if the scientific community has been willing to accept that the vastness of the universe originated from a single cosmic egg, than accepting and affirming limitations on our own potential seems patently absurd.

However, while directing our attention to the Single Cause liberates us from obsessive entanglements with the material world, we (within our embodiments) remain subject to its laws. We know that, in the physical world, every action generates an equal and opposite reaction. This law restores the state of balance, a concomitant to entropy. This precept is, however, in direct opposition to the non-physical, or the potential universe. While in the physical reality the *opposites* attract each other, in the causative world *like attracts like*.

Example.

A man and a woman are attracted to each other—although they clearly exhibit physical (sexual, appearance etc.), psychological (conscious and subconscious levels), and emotional (behavior patterns, emotive reactions etc.) opposites.(2) Yet, at the *intangible* level, knowingly or not, they foster the same or at least similar interests. They may find joy, amusement, pleasure in similar pursuits; perhaps they share interests in art, music, literature, any of the less "material" facets of life. In other words, the attraction of the opposites in the material is balanced by the attraction of the similarities in the realm of the immaterial. If their mutual attraction towards the compatible intangibles remains strong, their relationship will flourish. They will overcome, together, seemingly insurmountable difficulties, which external conditions throw at them. That which is indestructible, must, by definition, outlast that which is transient. They may fight over a host of unimportant, transient, inconsequential items that proliferate their everyday life. But what unites them is infinitely more powerful. It is that which is the glue of the invisible (the inexhaustible, the potential) universe.

If we are united above, we remain united below.

The singularity of the Cause is our indestructible bond. Theoretically, the same could be said of the opposites, but the chances that two people would share a preponderance of material interests, which would not infringe at each other's egocentric boundaries, is stacked heavily against them. They would live in a state of constant competition. Moreover, the "material" is not only limited but in a state of constant ferment.

Marriage is usually associated with children. Yet the love parents display towards their progeny is a manifestation of an instinct shared by all animals of higher order: a built-in programming designed to propagate the species.(3) For all who are preoccupied with the various means of controlling masses, i.e. the governments, churches, socio-economic conglomerates, marriage is a system of providing future labor force, taxes, charitable donations—all aimed at sustaining those already in power. To all of the above, marriage is very important institution. After all, no larger organization can survive without it.

On the other hand, for those among us who seek liberation, marriage is the first step in the journey from the ego-oriented to the Whole-oriented state of consciousness. The love we express towards the intangible is uniquely human. For us, marriage is a workshop, a marvelous opportunity for this very pursuit.

A real marriage.

For those among us who abide in this world (though, perhaps, think of ourselves not really of it), marriage is a magnificent laboratory wherein we can study the "law". We learn that the greater our "intangible" union, the greater may loom the "apparent" problems caused by the unavoidable attraction of the opposites. Those problems are, of course, not real. They appear genuine at the time of their manifestation, but, unless artificially maintained, or fed with false, emotional fuel, they dissipate into oblivion—when left alone. They are part of the transient, ephemeral, illusory, material reality. Knowing this law, this "secret", puts an end to sleepless nights, to endless arguments, to headaches and upset stomachs. What is left is the impalpable attraction, that which brought the man and the woman together to start with, and that which gave them countless moments of joy, pleasure, happiness and laughter.

There is one other aspect of marriage normally ignored. We are told that whenever two people find agreement on any subject whatsoever, this accord will activate the Universal Creative Life Force which makes all things possible.(4) The dyad is the minimum number of minds necessary to convert the subjective into objective reality.

But we must all remain vigilant.

No power on earth will keep a "couple of opposites" together, if they loose that which brought them together initially, that which united them at the deeper, the intangible level. Some may think of this initial attraction as falling in love, some refer to it as a karmic bond, others will relegate it to fate. To me, it is the cohesive action of the single Cause. It is the universal glue that tends to unite all into One, which gathers lost sheep into a single fold, which nudges the countless effects towards their Origin. This strange, wondrous attraction is sometimes called Divine Love.

***
980109

FOOTNOTES

1. Within an enclosed system such as the universe, entropy always increases and available energy decreases. By contrast, the spiritual realm is open-ended.
2. Contrary to popular belief, the mental and emotional realms are part of the material universe.
3. Clearly visible in all mammals, but also observed at ornithological and even at piscine levels
4. Matthew 18:19.

35
FEAR

In the darkest of nights, the wind blew out his torch. He lost his footing. Struggling to recover, he slipped over the precipice. In desperation—he grabbed wildly. His hand, drenched in fear, closed around a root of a tree poised over the chasm. For a while, fear gave him inhuman strength. Finally, he could hold on no longer.
He let go...
All went black.

He came to just as dawn was breaking. He was lying on a three-foot ledge. To his right was a drop of a thousand feet. Just above him—a root he held onto for his life. When he let go, he dropped less than a foot. He feared again of what might have been.

What do we fear?
The unknown. Always the unknown.
Yet it is not so simple. We fear not only the illusory dangers of an unknown future, but we fear, just as intensely, the past. Neither fear could overtake us, if we learned to live in the present. Why can't we? What is it within us, within our psyche, which continually displaces us from the only reality worth living?
Let us dissect this concept of fear.
And it is merely a concept because it is not grounded in reality. Fear based in the past manifests as resentment. Fear based in the future, foments anxiety. Neither has any bearing on the present. What we can experience in the present is

fright, which is a natural, spontaneous, intuitive reaction of the body to anything upsetting its equilibrium.

Fairly recently I found courage to start reading the Koran.(1) I said "courage" for no other reason than that my particular copy boasts 700 pages. Shorter than the Bible, but the Bible had not been written by one man. Furthermore I half expected to be at odds with the, as yet unknown, content.

Indeed, I was. On the first few dozen pages, the messenger (Mohammed) assured me, up to three times per page, that I was in imminent danger of repeated terrible, humbling, painful, if not eternal, fiery chastisements. Simultaneously, and in the context understandably, I have been as often admonished to fear God. I could not figure out whether to love this Deity, or to be scared witless of Him. By the time I turned some 200 pages, I began to realize that the fear tactic must have been directed at the children of Ishmael who, at the time, worshipped numerous Meccan shrines, (as well as the sun, moon, stars and some 360 idols, one for each day of the year). I dare say, such drastic circumstances forced the prophet to take drastic measures.

Frankly, for anyone who professes to believe in God who, in whatever form, personifies or symbolizes or expresses the Ineffable Essence of all perfections, fear is a contradiction in terms. How can we fear a Force, Being if you prefer, Who created the universe, surrounded us with breathtaking beauty, granted us awareness, and, most of all, gave us the ability to experience the ecstasy of Love? How can we fear such a Being? Sooner a bird should fear to fly, a fish—to dive into the ocean. Can a man fear life when Life Itself has chosen him to be Its mode of being?

Fear is an absurd concept.

How can we fear the past when the past brought us here? How can we fear the future when the past future resulted in such glorious present? How can we fear the present when we embody the indestructible consciousness indivisible from its Eternal Source?

And then I discovered my error. What Moses, Isaiah, David, Solomon, even as Mohammed, advocated was not fear at all.

It was reverence.

As my mind rests upon That which has the ability to create countless galaxies, to fashion complex elements in the hearts of stars for the embodiment of life yet to come... to that Force I am too drawn to fear. And as the Ineffable regards Its own works through my body's mortal eyes, granting me, perchance, a misty reflection of Its glory—then also I am too entranced to fear... And as I stand, starry eyed, in the deep silence of a cloudless night, the Ineffable displays before me the splendor of Its creation.... I am filled with enchantment, gratitude, overwhelming love. And reverence.

Never fear.

Whatever Being, Source, Creative Life Force, chooses to share with me, a lump of clay, Its inexhaustible potential... how could I fear It?

If I could but tear myself away from Its wonder, Its abundance, Its absurd effulgence of Love... perhaps then I could fear It. But then, I would surely die.

***
970120

FOOTNOTES

1. THE KORAN INTERPRETED, A translation by A.J. Arberry. [Touchstone, New York 1996].

*All metaphysics and theology—
all kinds knowledge,
in fact, and all the arts—
are like measuring the sea with a cup.
To find the Pearl demands a wholly different attitude.*

Jalal-ud-Din-Rumi
LIGHT UPON LIGHT, Inspirations from RUMI,
translated and adapted by Andrew Harvey,
North Atlantic Books, California 1996

36
LOOPHOLES

When lying on his deathbed, W. C. Fields, the mellifluous actor, comic, and reputedly affirmed atheist, had been asked what was he doing thumbing through a Bible. He replied: "Looking for loopholes."

And well he might.

The world is replete with them. It is up to us to find them.

In a way, each miracle is a loophole. It does not contradict the laws of nature, it suspends them. It suspends reality, as we know it to introduce a new version of it. Today, no self-respecting scientist, particularly physicist or astrophysicist would deny the existence of Black Holes. Yet... no one had ever seen one, no one measured nor even defined one. The best we can do is to observe the effects they have on the surrounding universe. Furthermore, the scientists claim that all known laws of physics are suspended within their domain. It's like saying that Black Holes are in, but not of this world. Note that neither saints, mystics nor theologians make such statements, but hard-nosed scientists.

And so it is with miracles.

Time and space are momentarily suspended and then hard-nosed skeptics, who, nevertheless, continue to reject them, observe their effects. They always will. All they can observe are the conditions before and after. No one can see the miracle itself. It takes place "elsewhere". It is not subject to laboratory conditions.

No more than a Black Hole.

Science teaches us that we cannot move an object of any mass whatever, faster than light. The reason is that at such a velocity the mass of the object would become infinite. Should we be within a spaceship travelling at such an impossible velocity (300,000 kilometers per second), we would be squashed to a sub-atomically thin wafer in the direction of travel and spread across the whole universe at right angles to it. We would be both: nowhere and everywhere. An uninspiring prospect. But we needn't worry. To achieve such a speed we would require infinite source of propulsion. An infinite power source. In other words, we would need to burn up the whole universe in order to propel a single atom.

Have you noticed how often the word infinite occurs in such discussions?

To my knowledge, the word "infinite" is expressed mathematically as ∞, or semantically as God. There is no other infinity that I am aware of. Until recently, mathematical consequences resulted only in defining limitations. But then, some wise man began looking for loopholes. Since sound is a wave, a vibration, and does not have any mass, the wise man decided to break with it the "light barrier". Frankly I do not understand how he did it, but the last I heard he was propelling sound-waves at five times the velocity of light. So what? So sound-waves can carry information. And, you might argue, our genetic code is information. Follow me....?

And this brings us right back to God.

All the great mystics, the "God scientists", always claim that it is we, you and I, who choose to live within a universe of limitations. We choose to identify with the created, not with the Creator. They claim that God is infinite and that we are the microcosm of the macrocosm; that there is an identical divine quality within us as without us; that "I and my Father are one".

We often seem to forget how "unnatural" (biological and/or zoological) life is. Nature, left to herself, tends to dissipate her energies towards an all-pervasive chaos. She is progressing toward a state known as an ultimate "maximum entropy", or "heat-death".(1) It is a condition wherein no energy can be used because it would be uniformly distributed throughout the cosmos. As life needs energy, it would cease––as would light, warmth, movement. No cause, no effect.

Time itself would come to a halt.

It would seem that in this ocean of chaos, all matter would be subject to a completely random distribution. No order, no laws, no beauty, and no hope. No love. Just omnipresent chaos. Whether we are subject to this fate or to a Gigantic Crunch (the opposite of the Big Bang), the prospect is unnerving.(2)

Unless....

Unless there is something which is outside the bounds of the manifested universe which is *not* subject to its laws. Like a Black Hole. Or God. Since a Black Hole would most assuredly carry a local equivalent of a Bright (?) Crunch, I prefer to settle for God. Why? Because God is a loophole which frees us from all the known laws of the universe. God is the agency that allows us to step outside the laws of thermodynamics, or any other laws, and affect such changes to reality as we, or God, see fit. This fact is amply illustrated by saviors, mystics, saints, healers, dervishes, Sufis, savants, and all who refuse to accept material limitations imposed on or by the universe.

This in no way implies that we should ignore the laws.

Once in this world we are all equally subject to its indomitable precepts. What we can do, however, all of us, is to step outside the material reality. We can choose to recognize that "life is a rare and unreasonable thing." That "the continuance of life depends on the maintenance of an unstable situation."(3) That life is a situation continually requiring new energy to exist. We can refuse to identify with the seemingly material, seemingly solid, the unstable—and see ourselves as controllers of the energy flows which *result* in the creation of matter. We can become the suppliers, or the agents for the supply, of fresh energy into the decaying universe. The matter, once created, would be subject to laws. We would not. We would continue to manipulate the atoms in such a way as to alter the reality. All by using the loopholes.

And, we are told, the greatest loophole of all is faith.

If we believe hard enough in anything, we can make it happen. Not by working our fingers to the bone. Not by gaining at someone else's expense. Not by developing ulcers worrying about our dubious chances for success. All we must do is accept that there is an Agency *outside* (as well as within) the observable universe that has the power, the ability, to overcome the second law of thermodynamics. Some call this power God. Others refer to It as the Universal Creative Life Force. Jalal-ud-Din Rumi, a mystic, poet, philosopher, has a different name for this loophole. He calls it neither power nor force. He simply calls it Love.

Try it.

***

980123

FOOTNOTES

1. The consequences of the 2nd law of thermodynamics are gleamed from THE UNIVERSE AND DR. EINSTEIN by Lincoln Barnett; [Signet Science Library, New York. pg. 103]
2. The latest on "chaos" theories denies this premise. They, the 'chaoists', claim that there is... order in their madness. It seems as though there is a *tendency* towards order even in chaos.
3. Watson, Lyall SUPERNATURE [Coronet Books, London 1974].

37
COSMOS

To most of us, "cosmos" means the world. To the Greeks, *kosmos* represents order, harmony, and even an ornament. Hence the world is the embodiment of a harmonious, orderly system. A thing of beauty. An ornament. What a pity that, according to our religions, such order, such harmonious beauty must come to an end.

God of the Hindus exhales the universe into existence, inhales—to end it. The Christians and the Moslem limit God's creative process to six days, while their Last Judgement dissolves the Cosmos with dire finality. Other faiths offer different versions of the Last Days, Fiery Demises and Gloomy Prospects. Every beginning is followed by a pendulous, dismal end. Even our scientists have joined the religious zealots with their Big Crunch theory.

What of the scale of their imaginings?

Most of the ancient prophets seemed confined to the earth as center of the universe. Their followers grew up in the solar system. Our parents stood in awe of the grandeur of the Milky Way Galaxy. Today, we count galaxies in billions. In 1966 the observable Universe measured 25 billion light-years—a diameter nearly four times that deemed correct as late as 1950.(1) Dare we limit the... limitless?

The Big Bang of the astrophysicists, the scriptures of the various religions, all suffer from an intrinsic duality. They acclaim monotheism, yet affirm good *and* evil. Reward and punishment. Our sciences are floating within relativity—with no absolutes, our religions are stuck in duality—within absolutes. Surely, monotheism should result in a *single* Force, not a mishmash of good and bad. If God means Good and is *omnipresent*, then there is no room for evil. Or, to put it bluntly, anyone advocating the existence of evil is denying the existence of God.

But what of those who aspire to be in this world but not of it?(2) They don't need the dichotomizing doctrine to sleep at night. They are quite happy not to place limitations on their God, their Cosmos, or anything else. Their Love is limitless; their Life is eternal their understanding need be contained neither by logic nor reason. They say that their God is beyond such trifles. To them, the Cosmos is the Face of God.(3) Eternal?

Luckily, there is another astrophysical theory called "continuous creation". An English cosmologist E. A. Milne suggested that the universe is generally uniform. He termed this the "cosmological principle". This principle seems to require an infinite universe.(4) Einstein used this assumption in his calculations, yet has shown that the universe can be finite in volume and yet contain an infinite number of galaxies.

The genius of Einstein!

Let us recap. The scientists gave us a Big Bang, necessitating a Big Crunch (otherwise we would drift away from each other forever). We also have a universe that is finite in volume yet limitless in terms of matter therein. How come?

The answer lies in the way we regard the universe. We are used to thinking of cosmos as countless galaxies, each containing countless stars with their planetary appurtenances (that's us, our tiny earths and suchlike). All the galaxies, according to the scientists, are hurling through space at flabbergasting velocities into the black abyss. We know this by measuring the "red shift".(5) Now imagine that all the galaxies, while whirling merrily around their own centers of gravity, are standing perfectly still in relation to each other. What gives the impression of movement is the *expansion of space*. If the stars on one side of earth were getting closer, and on the other drifted away, all would be well. But since they *all* seem to be leaving our environs in a lurch, then... we must be the centers of the world! The original nest-egg. The navel in God's belly. In fact this is what Aristotle and the Catholic Church thought and taught for some two millennia. Now the churches waver under pressure of the scientific community. The evolutionary theory, the Big Bang and other digestive problems are taken as fact. Alas, in truth, we are an insignificant star close to the outer edge of an average galaxy. We are tiny fish in a tiny pond...

Ouch!

Yet since the stars and galaxies do continue to increase their distance from us, we must accept that *space itself is expanding.*

So instead of a Big Bang, we may have countless smaller ones. Instead of a beginning and an end, we have countless adjustments, rather like seasons in a cosmic year. There is absolutely no need to demand singularity of location of this Bang. Since all space expands, we can have any number of bangs and all the spaces created thereby would be expanding. No matter where you find yourself within the confines of your or any other universe (or galaxy), all other systems would be moving away from you.

Why is this so important?

Because Cosmos is a thing of beauty. An ornament. It is the embodiment of harmony and order. I refuse to destroy it in a Big Crunch. I hope, so does God. After all, it's His creation. Any number of Little Bangs need not upset the overall balance. As I already said, it would be a question of cosmic seasons. Or seasons on a cosmic scale. We know there are countless Black Holes, which absorb and remove from our universe all the unwanted, spent matter; perhaps to be cleansed, perhaps irradiated in the infernal fires of unbelievable pressures—only to be released back into the Cosmos, when ready. Actually space too is sucked into the Black Holes together with all material debris. The gravity is known to cause the curvature of space. Gargantuan gravity would result in the collapse of space altogether—locally—say over a few million light-years.

Perhaps this is the latent memory we carry of the infernal Hell's fire...

Now, with all those Black Holes vacuuming our space, we need the counter-action of Continuous Creation. And who does the creating? Believe it or not... you and I are the creators. You and I are extensions, or instruments, or channels through which the continuous process of creation goes on.

And on.

And on....

We are immortal.

Of course, we are not yet at the level of evolution to cause supernovae. But there may well be others, vastly more advanced beings, who designate massive stars to recycle their matter into some new worlds. The exploding supernova of 1054 is now known as the Crab Nebula. For the last 944 years it's space has been expanding. It already measures well over 6 light-years across. As the space continues to expand, we may witness whole galaxies collapsing into their Black Cores and then, perhaps, one day, going off in great cosmic bangs. God's fireworks. New worlds to evolve new intelligences, new creative channels to sustain the creative process. Isn't this what God might be doing?

Cosmos. God's ornament.

No true lover of Life, of the Creative Life Force, could conceive of a total annihilation of Its Manifestation. We can transmute Its elements from one to another, we can compress or expand the intensity of Its action, we can release It into the vastness of space, but we can never, never, destroy It. Our minds will forever strive to grasp the vastness of Its Presence, but only our hearts will help us understand Its works.

In spite of his genius, Einstein failed to arrive at the Unified Field Theory, which would bridge the gap between the uncertainty principle of Quantum Mechanics and his own orderly Theory of Relativity [or a single law that would govern the micro and the macrocosm]. Such a law would describe and define a force, which would have to satisfy the exigencies of an "expanding" universe (offering unlimited freedom), as well as gather and hold the vastness of the Cosmos together. A seemingly impossible task for a single agency. Yet, over thousands of years, to the many mystics who have graced the human race, such a force always existed.

It is known to them as Divine Love.

***
980127

FOOTNOTES

1. Light year is the distance a photon travels in a "vacuum", in 365 days at 300,000 kilometers per second. The universe observable in 1966 was thus measured as 60 x 60 x 24 x 365 x 300,000 x 25,000,000,000 kilometers in diameter, or approx. 236,520,000,000,000,000,000,000 km. It has grown since.

2. John 15:19

3. In the Koran it is written, "wherever you turn, there is the Face of God". [Light upon Light, Inspirations from RUMI, Andrew Harvey, North Atlantic Books, California.]

4. Otherwise, when reaching the edge, we would have uniformity on one side and zilch on the other.

5. As the source of light recedes from us, the successive light waves are pulled further apart. The wavelengths thus become longer than normal, and the entire spectrum is shifted towards the red end. It is the opposite of the "violet shift" when the shortening of the wavelength causes them to shift towards the violet end of the spectrum.

NOTE: Since writing this essay, the theoretical physicists came up with a multi-universe concept, which has its being within at least eleven dimensions. Don't give up hope. Einstein thought it to be infinite and, not that it matters, so do I.

God doesn't play dice with the universe.

Albert Einstein

*I am the Self, seated in the hearts of all creatures.
I am the beginning, the middle,
and the end of all beings.*

BHAGAVAD-GITA

38
SUBMISSION

Islam means submission, surrender, utter obedience.

To what? To whom? Why?

The answer is by no means clear.

If it were, there would not be an exuberant proliferation of imams, who continue to impose their narrow-minded, dogmatic, inflexible, fundamentalist interpretations of the Koran on the only slightly more ignorant, easy to manipulate, masses. In spite of the aseptic Islamic leaders, over the centuries Islam provided better opportunities for propagating an inner doctrine than any of its religious precursors.(1)

This inner doctrine of the Koran seems to have contributed to the wisdom of the Sufis, while remaining hidden to most Moslem believers—even as the inner knowledge of the Bible appears inaccessible to the vast majority of Christians. At first, perhaps second and third, reading, the Koran defines the believers' relationship to God in terms of fear, at best as unconditional, overpowering, and inundating reverence. The New Testament attempts to define this same relationship in terms of love. You don't fear that which you love. It is hard to love that which you fear. By all accounts there is little love in the Koran of the fundamentalists. The word love does not appear in the index to the Book. On the other hand there is hardly a page wherein thoroughly unpleasant, painful, terrible, fiery, vengeful chastisements are not proffered and reiterated with never-ending enthusiasm. Strangely enough, an All-forgiving, All-clement, All-compassionate God wields this ghastly chastisement upon us. The paradigm of the carrot and the stick? No wonder the Islamic world foments in a state of confusion. The turmoil in Algeria, Egypt, Palestine, Iran, Pakistan, India, Afghanistan.... One billion people—seemingly lost.

Such is the Koran. In the Name of God, the Merciful, the Compassionate.

And yet...

And yet, Jalal-ud-Din Rumi calls upon the Koran and the Prophet many-a-time. Since the day of Christ there has been no greater advocate, indeed champion, of love than Rumi. And Rumi quotes the Koran. A mystery? He claims that there are seven levels of understanding the Koran. I might well believe this. It took me over twenty years to begin understanding the inner symbolism of the Torah and the Gospels. Twenty years of daily study. We never stop learning. Some hardly began. Some are still dead.

Yet I found the God of Islam so resplendent, so absolute, and so incredibly inaccessible that He couldn't be loved; He can only be revered. He, Allah, never leaves His heavenly abode—except to inflict chastisement. Paradise is only for the dead. By contrast, the God of Christ is incredibly accessible: "I and my Father are one." The God of the Bible is as close as the innermost chamber of your heart.

Many, many, years before Mohammed was born, a different Prophet knew what Mohammed never discovered: "For unto us a child is born..." wrote Isaiah, "and the government shall be upon his shoulder: and his name shall be called Wonderful, Counsellor, The Mighty God..."(2) This God is no less resplendent, no less merciful, but his "chastisement" (surely the favorite word in the Koran), He leaves to lesser gods. Later, Rumi points out, "Everyone of us has a Jesus within him, waiting to be born".(3)

A present day writer-teacher, Deepak Chopra, reiterates: "Remember... deep inside every one of us there is a God in embryo. It has only one desire. It wants to be born." One day we shall all submit to this God. We shall not be forced, coerced, threatened, chastised into servile obedience.

We shall be lured into It by Infinite Love.

And thus, I doubt if there are many who can truly submit to the God of Koran; one God, Allah, never to be born and reborn within our hearts, our souls. Rumi also believes in but one God. Nor does he in any way affirm the divinity of Jesus. What he does affirm is the divine reality of love personified by Jesus. The Koran affirms the reality of chastisement. On and on and on.

R. A. Nicholson, in his *Literary History of the Arabs*, writes: "The preposterous arrangement of the Koran is mainly responsible for the opinion almost unanimously held by European readers that it is obscure, tiresome, uninteresting; A farrago of long-winded narratives and prosaic exhortations, quite unworthy to be named in the same breath with the Prophetical Books of the Old Testament."(4) Professor A. Guillaume in *Islam*, (Penguin Books), writes "The Koran is one of the world's classics which cannot be translated without grave loss. It has a rhythm of peculiar beauty and a cadence that charms the ear. ...read aloud or recited it has an almost hypnotic effect..."(5)

Read aloud *in Arabic*.

I can sympathize with this thesis. I love Italian opera, sung in Italian, although I do not speak the language of Verdi, Bellini, Puccini or Rossini. Yet, I love opera dearly, I admire its intrinsic, sometimes almost hypnotic beauty. Such beauty one can almost revere; alas, I have no desire to make a religion out of Italian operas. Someone made a religion out of the Koran. Could it be that they were so taken by the "rhythm of peculiar beauty", so enamoured with the "cadence that charms the ear" that they (even as I did with Italian opera) chose to ignore the lyrics? If music be the food of love....(6)

Yet Rumi quotes *the words*. So do other Sufis. And they were mystics. Students of the divine, the transcendent.

About a year ago, a doctor removed a few cells, which have been forced into a cycle of division through an act of violence imposed by a single sperm invading a woman's womb.(7) A cycle of division initiated by a vicious act of rape. For his act of mercy, the doctor has been murdered by a misguided fundamentalist, supposedly a Christian. [Similar crimes had been committed since by ardent "Christians" in the name of Jesus].

A year later, a convicted murderer knelt down in the center of the Afghan capital's national stadium field, to await being executed by the brother of the victim. More than 35,000 male residents of Kabul attended the execution.(8) Mohammed counted Jesus of Nazareth among the Messengers of God. In fact the Prophet of Islam wrote: Say: *'People of the Book, you do not stand on anything, until you perform the Torah and the Gospel, and what was sent down to you from your Lord.'* (9) The Gospel? The sublime teaching of love and forgiveness? And the Koran continues to echo the Torah: A *life for a life, an eye for an eye, a nose for a nose...* *...but whosoever forgoes it as a freewill offering, that shall be for him an expiation.*(10)

Or... let him who is without sin cast the first stone.

There is little to choose between the Afghan fundamentalists and the witnesses, surely no fewer in number, we find in Lynchburg, Virginia. The Moslem fundamentalist confused animal justice with divine mercy. His Christian counterpart confused a human embryo with an immortal soul. Both killers, "executioners", claim to be absolved by their stern, hateful, exacting God. Indeed, *their* God, they claim, is but One God. The only one they are aware of. A very different God from the image shown us by the Prince of Peace.

The Gospel states that God judges no man(11), Judgments are left to the misguided ones in Kabul or in

Virginia. Both stem from complete ignorance of the teaching of the Great Messengers of God. One God. The Merciful, the Compassionate One.

Whatever religion. Whatever age

***
980317

FOOTNOTES

1. Shah, Idries THE SUFIS [Doubleday & Co. Inc., New York 1964].
2. Isaiah 10:6
3. LIGHT UPON LIGHT, Inspirations from RUMI, by Andrew Harvey, [North Atlantic Books, Berkeley, California]. (pg. 110)
4. The KORAN Interpreted, A translation by A.J. Arberry, [Simon & Schuster].
5. ibid.
6. TWELFTH NIGHT, William Shakespeare, Act 1.
7. Fetal cells continue to divide for the whole duration of pregnancy. An adult body numbers about 10^{28} cells. [That's 100, 000, 000, 000, 000, 000, 000, 000, 000, 000 cells]
8. Reported by Gazette, Montreal, Saturday, March 14, 1998. Pg. A 26.
9. The KORAN Interpreted, A translation by A.J. Arberry; Sura V/72, 'The Table'
10. ibid. SuraV / 49
11. John 5:22

NOTE
(1999)

Twenty-one months after I wrote the essay "Submission", on October 20, 1999 an event took place that could well change the face of Islam. Abdurrahman Wahid was elected President of Indonesia. A devout Muslim, he is far removed from the grotesque extreme fundamentalism so prevalent in other parts of the world. When Moslem leaders joined in the condemnation of the author Salman Rushdie, Wahid stood alone in his defense. When other Moslem leaders condemned Israel, he visited Jerusalem to accept a prize in honor of the assassinated Yitzhak Rabin. Wahid preaches religious tolerance within the world's largest Muslim nation.

[*My optimism had proven premature. On 23 July 2001, the MPR (People's Consultative Assembly) unanimously voted to impeach Wahid and to replace him with Megawati as President*].

"*It is necessary to note that opposite things work together, even though nominally opposed*"

Jalal-ud-Din Rumi
[Fihi Ma Fihi]
"In It What Is In It"

39
TITHING

Like all actions affecting the course of human events, giving, taking or sharing, can result in either good or bad consequences for which we, the givers, takers or sharers, must bear a degree of responsibility.

Beware of tithing!

Many, many years ago, there was a nation of people who thought that their spiritual life was of no lesser importance than the mundane demands of their physical bodies. Since spiritual pursuits have been regarded as non-productive, the ancients devised a system wherein ninety percent of the citizens would donate one-tenth of their income for the upkeep of the remaining ten percent of the people. Luckily, their nation consisted of ten tribes. Nine tribes would support the remaining clan, which would devote all its efforts toward the spiritual upkeep of the whole nation.

Later they learned that their original definition of productivity had been very wrong. They learned that those dedicated to spiritual matters can actually feed 5000 men (beside women and children) with five loaves of bread and a couple of fish. Since, however, the priesthood (supported by nine-tenth of the population) was, by then, firmly established, this insidious information was duly ignored. Tithing, as they called their taxation system, was as well entrenched in their society as it is in ours, today. By the 20th century, ties of blood no longer united the clan of non-productive people. Furthermore, the original 'tithe', meaning 'a tenth', grew progressively to well over 50% of the hard-earned income of the productive people. Today, the money is no longer used for the propagation of spiritual matters. It is *mis*used for countless totally useless objectives, designed explicitly to keep those wielding power—in power. The new tribe, clan or gang became known as "the civil servants" or, generically, "the government".

There is one other group that specializes in living at the expense of others.

Since one-tenth of the population no longer keeps itself preoccupied with the matters of God, tithing, in its traditional sense, makes no sense. Yet, there are countless mountebanks, masquerading under the guise of various religions, who encourage tithing. Furthermore, they are no longer satisfied with tithing nine times their own number. They try to collect a tithe from thousands upon thousands of television viewers, to bolster their obscene private coffers. Some such charlatans have already been brought to justice. Many others are still at large.

The original concept of tithing once held a more noble purpose.

It had been designed to teach people that material welfare is a fluid concept. That true wealth, like water, tends to find its lowest level. For those amongst us who do not derive any of our income from any arm of any government, tithing means *giving away a part of our income without any strings attached.* This last qualification is of utmost importance. Unless we qualify our donations this way, we bear the resultant Karma. Unless our gift is completely unconditional, we remain co-responsible with the recipient, for the good or bad, which might result from such a donation. And the consequences can be very serious. I am reminded of the reports that the charitable donations directed at the famine in Ethiopia (officially for starving children) have been responsible for prolonging the war by ten years.

The ancient desert dwellers did not divulge their secret knowledge regarding the benefits of tithing. It took us centuries, perhaps millennia, to learn that the real purpose of giving, of sharing one's good fortune, is not so much to help others as to help oneself. That the only way to gain wealth— is to give wealth. The only way to gain love—is to give love. Like attracts like. We can never be sure whether, when giving, we really help the recipient. I'm reminded of a story of two Buddhists taking a meditative stroll along a busy sidewalk. The younger aspirant noticed a snail making it's torturous way across the pavement. Lest a pedestrian might inadvertently step on the poor creature, the younger monk picked it up, and gently deposited it on the other side of the sidewalk. His Master, wise in the ways of the world, remarked: "Do you know, my friend, this snail spent three days and three nights on the verge of this sidewalk, trying to gather enough courage to cross it. Now, he'll have to start all over again."

This story might be taken lightly, but there are countless examples of gifts resulting in as much harm as good. The papers are full of reports wherein the gift of the freedom to bear arms resulted in multiple deaths. Wherein the gift of money resulted in drug abuse. Wherein the gift of a vehicle, before responsibility has been learned, resulted in maiming or death of an innocent bystander.

Giving is not an easy matter.

There is one other aspect of tithing that needs examination. According to the Canadian Center for Philanthropy, as of mid 1997, in Canada (alone) there have been 75,000 charities registered for tax-deductible status. This figure is growing at the rate of about 1,500 each year. Collecting for these organizations is a growing number of professional firms. A CBC News program [The Magazine(1)] reported that an average of 26% of the money collected is allocated to "expenses" associated with raising the money. The total collected has been reported as $90 Billion. I can only imagine that this vast sum is due to large corporations writing off considerable sums for promotional gains.

Do you wish to know who benefits from *your* generosity? The no-strings-attached policy is now under a considerable strain.

So we might as well stop pretending that we give in order to benefit others. When we receive begging letters from professional usurpers, we give in order to lessen our feeling of guilt—no matter how misplaced. And we should give. Give plenty. We should share as much of our wealth as we possibly can. Not because we feel guilty for having been blessed with riches. Not even to benefit others. We must give because giving is the greatest pleasure a man can have. The greatest joy we can experience.

But let us not say that our gifts are only for feeding the hungry or helping the poor. After all, being poor, like any and all other conditions of life, is but a state of consciousness. And we cannot change the state of consciousness in anther person. This feat can only be achieved from within. If it were otherwise, all people would radiate the love of Jesus, the detachment of Buddha, the wisdom of Lao Tsu. The best we can hope for is to give from the richness of our hearts, not merely our bank accounts. What matters is the act of sharing, of being one with the rain, the sunshine, which benefits the good and the bad, alike. Giving, we enrich the fabric of the manifested universe. In the instant of sharing we become one with the Infinite Source.

With no strings attached.

True gifts never really come from one person to another. They come from the realm of unbounded potential, from the inexhaustible spring of Life, which gushes, eternally, within our hearts. We are no more than channels, passing on a little of what we have learned.

***
980331

FOOTNOTE

1. The Magazine, Channel 6, 10 p.m., October 13, 1999. [These data have been added later].

40
FUNDAMENTALISM

There is a great misunderstanding regarding this term, as referred to religious interpretation of reality. I have friends who think that anyone who believes that God created Adam in 4004 BC is a fundamentalist. They are right, but only in part. What makes such believers fundamentalists is not their literal interpretation of the Bible, but their conviction that the Bible had been written about, and addressed, the physical, or material reality. The fundamentalist's need is fed by an unquenchable hunger for the permanent, for that which they can fall back on, rely on, within a world of unpredictable, sudden and constant change. They hunger for irrefutable facts regarding their existence. For a haven within the swirling turmoil of material reality. Alas, if there is one law controlling this realm which is more adamant than any other, it is the law of change. Without it, biological life could not exist.

Looking for *anything* permanent within the *material* universe denies the very nature of this universe.

In essence, whether we believe that the human race is 6,000 or 6,000,000 year old is *of no consequence*. Likewise, it is of little import whether we believe that Moses parted the waters of the Red Sea, or that Jesus converted water into first quality wine... although this last trick I would very much like to learn. What matters is: how our beliefs affect our state of consciousness *at this very moment*—as this instant of eternity is the only instant in which we are in touch with that aspect of us which is immortal. Soul, the biblical El, the individualized Spirit, the Higher Self (call It what you like), has Its being only in the present. It has Its being beyond space, beyond time.

You are not a fundamentalist because you interpret the Bible literally. You interpret the Bible literally (even in small part) because you are a fundamentalist.

If your reality is centered in the material world—you are a fundamentalist. If you are concerned with your past or future—you are a fundamentalist: you exemplify a half-life; you are not yet awake, or, as Jesus put it: you are still dead. You suffer from an illusion. Yes... you probably really suffer. The pope John-Paul II writes about "the law of suffering,"(1) of the "mystery of suffering and death."(2) Your suffering, indeed the necessity of suffering, is so ably advocated by all who define us as sinners in danger of eternal hellfire. Recognize heaven and hell as states of consciousness and suffering dissipates. This very knowledge "fills with great joy."(3) Listening to countless preachers advocating the benefits of suffering, of the "purification" of soul through self denial, through abnegation, renunciation, fasting... I can but wonder if they ever noticed that the words "joy" or "rejoicing" appears in the Bible no less than 150 times! We have not been brought to this world to suffer, but to rejoice.

Unless we choose to be fundamentalists.

Unless we choose to believe in illusion.

The Buddha, Christ, Sai Baba and other avatars do not recognize the fundamental (material or physical) world, as real. Oh, they are well aware of the suffering ensuing from the misconception of the true reality. They even accept its *illusory* existence, but only as a point of reference for gathering experience by observing the consequences of divergent actions. Within the fundamental worlds, joy cannot exist without suffering—any more than shadow be cast without light, or sweetness experienced but in contrast to that which is bitter. We learn by comparing the opposites. If it weren't for the opposites, the physical worlds would not, could not, exist. Alas, the physical worlds are not... real.

If we can metabolize this truth, we shall we set free.

No compromise is possible on this issue. We cannot accept the teaching of the avatars in part only. Were we to do so, the dichotomy would lead us to an asylum. (It very often does). Either we recognize ourselves as spiritual entities—"detached" actors learning from the interplay of opposite actions, emotions, concepts, or we think of yourselves as material bodies, endowed with limited mental abilities, a nondescript-undefined-incomprehensible "soul", and unlimited capacity for suffering. If we choose the latter, we also choose to remain embroiled in a paradoxical existence, filled with "mysteries", in this "valley of tears". We must then also accept the concept of hell, the existence of evil, and the greatest perversion of all: the necessity of suffering.

We cannot serve two masters.(4)

For as long as people recognize the physical world as the sole reality, they will never understand the messages which the great avatars tried so hard to convey to us. As Sai Baba put it "life is only relatively real."(5) To think otherwise is to be a fundamentalist; it is to build one's belief system, one's existence, on false premises. It is to substitute an ephemeral, transient, dream for the essence of being. According to Sai Baba, life on earth is even less than a dream; it is but a memory of one. No sane person would preoccupy himself or herself, extensively, with a dream. We should learn from it all we can, and then get on with our lives. Now and in our next incarnation—and the following, ever unfolding, countless fragments of eternity. And between the incarnations we shall dream. We shall explore our infinite potentials. Until we learn. And then we shall go no more out.(6)

We are eternal dreamers. Whenever we awaken (some people call it dying), we look back and smile—in disbelief...

***
981117

FOOTNOTES

1. PAPAL WISDOM compiled by Matthew E. Bunson, [Penguin Group]. Sign of Contradiction 19.3.
2. EVANGELIUM VITAE, 67.
3. Compare John 15:11
4. Matthew 6:24
5. Schulman, Arnold BABA [Simon & Shuster, Canada]. While the teaching of Buddha and Jesus may well be shrouded in the mists of ages, Sai Baba was born in 1926.
6. Revelation 3:12

The individual is the only reality

Carl G. Jung
[Approaching the Unconscious]

41
AGING

It creeps up on us. Every action presents an ever-increasing effort. We seem to lack energy. We really do. We move about less and less—we like to stay in one spot, preferably our favorite armchair. The less we move the stiffer we become. The stiffer we become the less we move. We begin aging.

We don't like the way things are, but we resent change. We hold little tolerance for anyone who disagrees with us. We take their arguments as personal attacks. We dislike new concepts, ideas, or deviations from an established norm. We lose our sense of humor. (At least, everybody else does). Life has become very serious. We carry on our shoulders the wisdom of the ages. Youngsters... what do they know!? We completely forgot that Jesus, Mozart, Mendelssohn died before they reached forty—that Einstein made his earthshaking breakthroughs when he was twenty-six.

We keep forgetting....

No matter. So little happens in our lives. Recent events are hardly worth remembering. Our memory is perfect. We remember minute details from our distant past. Our childhood, even. Ah, those were the days... Providentially, we lose our perception of time. We go shopping for an hour; it feels like three—maybe longer. Time is precious yet indeterminate. The present loses its reality. We prefer the past.

What happened? Why are we still on this earth? Why do we cling to life? Why...

I don't remember... what was I going to ask?

Most of us think that aging is a process as inevitable as taxes. When we dwell on our aches and pains, we forget how we'd hurt the day after that first tennis match of the season—way back when... We don't want to remember. It would upset our self-indulgence. Our wallowing in: "surely... at my age..." attitude. We are firmly committed to growing infirm, mentally and physically, as if it had been written into the laws of the universe.

Is it? Are our bodies designed to deteriorate so badly while we still occupy them? Was it God, or Nature, who made such a preposterous design blunder?

Surely, *we* had no hand in it?

It's a question of viewpoint.

If we regard ourselves as (intelligent) animals then we remain subjects to the indomitable laws that govern the physical universe. We are designed to perform certain functions: to eat, defecate, breed, sleep and thus survive. We may or may not develop other agenda. We are assigned a specific number of heartbeats, our cells are endowed with the facility to divide and renew themselves a predetermined number of times.(1) Our internal organs will function perfectly for a comparative length of time until, one day, they will function no more. Unless someone eats us, or at any rate kills us, sooner: "before our time." When we die, the world will have been unaffected by our existence. It will be neither better nor worse.

It will be as if we have never lived.

But then, at a certain moment in our evolution a strange thing happens. We acquire the power to say no. We rebel until we get kicked out of Eden. We impose our will on the external environment in order to become independent of it.

The end of childhood?

It took us 100 million lifetimes to reach this stage.(2) Now, finally, we begin to assume responsibility for our existence. We make countless errors. We poison our pulmonary, cardiovascular, and even immune, systems in an attempt to control our lives; then we develop rudimentary medicine to counteract our blunders. We may be stupid but we are stubborn. We try hard, so hard we suffer stress—the greatest aging factor of them all. For a while, we are vibrant with energy. We feel we have been designed to conquer. The more we believe in ourselves the greater our glory. The greater our achievements. We develop sciences, religions, arts; we develop socio-political systems; we break up humanity into tribes, nations, and organizations to increase competition. We fight wars to prove that we are right. We reach for the unknown. We search for the fountain of youth. And, after all this, eventually, we still grow old. It is as though aging was an inevitable process, a sort of reversal of growing up. We are born with a self-centered view of the universe; we finish our lives with the same orientation. This year(3), in the USA, 1.6 million senior citizens await death in 16,700 nursing homes. By 2030, the number of people over 85 will double.

Will they be 85 years young?

In fact, aging has little to do with the number of years we hold under our belts. I've known "old" people who were born a mere 40 years earlier. I've known, and heard of, vibrant "youngsters" of a 100 and more. It's all a question of attitude.

We don't age because our bones creak. If physical dexterity were the determining factor, Stephen Hawking would have been dead long ago. Neither do we age because we live a certain number of years. We grow old because we *expect* to grow old. Perhaps this command became deeply encoded into our genes during those 100 million incarnations the Hindus talk about. This is not a paradox. Aging is a *mental* process. If man could believe hard enough that his body can be rejuvenated at will, it would be. It would not be a miracle. His body would simply respond to a natural creative process. The Old Testament purports that men once walked this earth upwards of a 1000 years.

Aging takes place in the mind.

When all decisions are made for us, *when we stop using our mind,* it atrophies. Loss of memory, inability to make decisions, lack of diverse interests, all lead to apathy in quick succession. I know of no one who's mental condition improved in an establishment designed for senior citizens.

And then, there is a quite different viewpoint.

For those of us who regard ourselves as states of consciousness, as spiritual entities, the process is quite different. Before we enter the bodies of our hosts, we spent "time" in *samadhi*, a trance like state in which we dream of infinite possibilities. We dream how to bring out the inner beauty into the outer realm. How to make it manifest.

When we awaken in physical bodies equipped with means of carrying out our mission, we too must learn to function in the worlds of matter. But we do not interfere with our host's prerogatives. To us the body, the man-woman, is not a "physical" entity; it is an assembly of atoms, of bits of energy endowed with intelligence of their own, with its own agenda. The body, the assembly of atoms, has acquired its intelligence or experience over millions of years. The constituent parts of the body are in a state of constant flux, a whirlwind of activity, wherein trillions of actions and reactions take place every second.

When asked, we whisper advice with a silent, insistent voice.

But we do not impose.

The body we share with its host is in total control over its universe, its reality. We stay with our hosts as long as possible. Sometimes they only listen to us when their physical functions deteriorate. When they grow "old". But even then... we love our hosts too much to impose. In a way, we made them what they are. In a way, they are our children.

We are here to help—and to observe.

***

981118

FOOTNOTES

1. In an article in TIME mag., Jan. 26, 1998, Christine Gorman states the following: 1 trillion cells in the human body contain their own biological clock. Telomeres, little bits of DNA that coat the tips of the chromosomes, much like the plastic cuffs of shoelaces, prevent the strands from unraveling. Every time a cell spits in two, the telomeres shorten, until finally, after about 40 to 90 divisions, they are reduced to stubs. Only an enzyme called telomerase, discovered in 1984, can repair the damaged telomeres.

2. The number of incarnations assigned to us according to old Vedic philosophies.

3. The essay was written in 1998

...a man should leave the world a better place
than when he came into it.
For no other reason was be born,
for no other reason does he die.

Sai Baba

*If you ask what is the single most important key to longevity,
I would have to say it is avoiding worry, stress and tension.
And if you didn't ask me,
I'd still have to say it.*

George Burns

42
BABEL

It never ceases to amaze me (an oft repeated phrase in my essays!) how a select clique of reputedly illustrious *cognoscenti* succeeds in gathering together in order to spew, on unsuspecting public, such voluminously machinated nonsense.

Umberto Eco begins his latest book with a contrived premise, which he then proceeds to develop with ultra logical reasoning. Regrettably, what works well in Sci-Fi (or fantasy, such as his *Name of the Rose* or the *Foucault's Pendulum*)(1) does not strike resonance in the "real world". Other European scholars join Dr. Eco in *The Making of Europe*, what promises to be a remarkably long-winded series on central themes in the history of European peoples and their cultures. Eco's contribution (with an oh... so impressive bibliography) is entitled In search for the perfect language.(2) All who plodded through the Foucault's Pendulum know what to expect.

The search for a perfect language is not a new hobby. Is seems to have tested such noble minds as Dante's, who claimed that Hebrew spoken in Eden was the perfect and inimitable example of such a language(3), while Maria Corti averred that "What God gave Adam was a set of principles of universal grammar."(4) To Eco, regression to pre-Babel days appears paramount to progression in his search for new horizons. I must admit, though, that Eco reports on the historical struggles at finding (or returning to) a perfect language (usually regarded as Hebrew) with a studiously disguised wink.

A perfect language understood as being capable of mirroring the true nature of objects (presumably, according to fundamentalists)(5) is, by definition, impossible. Objects are whole. They represent not just the spatial constrains endowed with particular characteristics, but an integral bundle of information contained in a specific conglomerate of atoms and subatomic particles, within a field of the attendant forces and energies. Atoms are all similar. Their arrangement as well as the number of their appurtenances (electrons etc) differs. A perfect language—i.e.: a laterally or linearly structured semantic description would require infinite volumes to define a single object.

Naming of the animals by Adam(6) describes the process of translating *gestält* concepts into symbols. But contrary to Maria Corti and all her misguided alter egos, it was *not* God who gave Adam the words, or the symbols, but it was Adam, who *gave names to all cattle, and to the fowl of the air, and to every beast of the field*, while God waited patiently "to see what he (Adam) would call them." Thus the presumed "perfect language", Hebrew or otherwise, did not originate with God, nor even with divine inspiration, but, to use imperfect semantics of the fundamentalists, with the primeval ultra-primitive illiterate called Adam.

Yet Dr. Eco's book explores the premise that since before the Tower of Babel there had been only one language, we can trace back our history, and find the great unifying factor, which, after Babel, had set us apart. Interesting idea, alas, as seems consistent with great scholars, who specialize in areas so narrow, they cannot see the forest for the trees.

Eco suffers from the same premise, as do many of his predecessors, whom he quotes diligently, i.e. that the Bible is a historical account of historical events recorded for posterity. And this he does in spite of his avowed awareness of Cabalistic interpretations of the Torah, who "use this instrument to uncover this reality..." and, that the text to be fully understood, must be regarded as "allegorical-philosophical, Hermetic and mystic." Having said so, he continues to ignore his own admonitions.

Let us take a stab at reality.

The Proverbs (18:10) state: The *name of the LORD is a strong tower*. Thus, in the Bible, a "tower"(7) intrinsically symbolizes a state of raised consciousness. While *Babel* means the *gate of God*, its location, i.e. *Babylon* symbolizes a state of confusion. Problems started when man began to lose distinction between a raised state of *spiritual* as against *mental* consciousness. Furthermore, the Tower of Babel had been built of brick(8), symbolizing an inferior material as compared to stone, even as intellect is inferior to spiritual awareness. In other words, the Tower of Babylon defines a condition wherein man thought that he could advance himself through his own, i.e. mental efforts. Such a course could only result in losing that which united us, i.e. the faith in a One God, or unity inherent in Spirit. Once the prerogatives of our egos supplant those of our soul, we can no longer advance in our spiritual evolution. Spirit is that which unites us, while the exigencies of ego set us apart. This is the lesson inherent in the parable of the Tower of Babel.

As for Adam naming all those beasts, it simply means that it is not spirit but mind or intellect that is capable of linguistically structured symbols. The spirit regards or recognizes all things by direct perception in a gestält fashion, rather as a baby perceives its mother's face as the source of all good.

And so Dr. Eco, and all his predecessors, appear to have started on the wrong foot. The multiplicity of languages, which they claim ensues from the biblical Babel, is only indicative of population growth and the attendant dispersion of people over vast areas in search of fresh hunting grounds. The gradual separation of warring tribes by ever growing distances was exacerbated by limited modes of transportation. Furthermore, as Abbé Pluche notes in his *La méchanique des langues et l'art de les einsegner* (1751), the fact that our forefathers developed different modes of communications further served to keep them apart, and thus reinforced the differentiation of languages.

So much for languages. Any languages.

As noted by Deepak Chopra, at preverbal level all nature speaks the same language. Also, at preverbal level (before Adam was "dressed in skin", i.e. came to inhabit a material body), duality was not a recognizable concept. Only eating of the "tree of knowledge", of good *and* evil, enabled us to acquire knowledge by observing the interplay of the opposites. Finally, at the preverbal level, we, at a deeper level, continue to communicate with the whole universe, we exchange knowledge, what the military call: "intelligence", in an ongoing, continuous, and uninterrupted fashion. On occasion we come across people who can extend this ability to their conscious level and thus control reality at will. When they do that, we call such actions miracles.

***

98112

FOOTNOTES

1. Umberto Eco's previous literary offerings (inter alia).
2. Eco, Umberto THE SEARCH FOR THE PERFECT LANGUAGE English translation. [© Blackwell Publ. 1995, Great Britain].
3. ibid. pg. 45
4. ibid. pg. 44
5. I regard as fundamentalist anyone who recognizes Maya (the phenomenal universe) as Reality. See essay no. 40 hereinbefore.
6. Genesis 2:19-20
7. Hebrew *migdal*
8. Genesis 11:3 et al.

'Babel' signifies what the name means—confusion.

There are times when we find ourselves in the confusion of the sense consciousness, and its thoughts are so strong that they seem to have us in complete subjugation. Such cases symbolize captivity in Babylon.

METAPHYSICAL BIBLE DICTIONARY
[Unity School of Christianity, Unity Village, Mo. Pg.92].

43
BLISS

If our life is punctuated with moments of blissful pleasure yet we cannot sustain such a state of consciousness for any length of time, we are not fulfilling our destiny. Only when we discover our specific purpose, our *dharma*, we can experience the bliss resulting from such a realization. Only then shall we abide in perfect harmony with the universe. Only then shall we manifest our unique talents. It will be as though we added the missing note to a vital chord. We shall achieve a sense of completeness.

We shall be drunk with bliss.

In the vastness of the universe, every one of us is a unique entity, neither superior nor subservient to any other. The anthropocentric theologies derived from Aristotelian, Ptolemaic, Hipparchusian and finally Christian philosophies (which placed man at the pinnacle of creation) are no longer valid. Likewise, the basic tenet of Enlightenment that man is the measure of all things, wielding supremacy over other forms of life, is challenged by the enormity of the observable universe, which science already expanded by millions of light-years. Yet, within this almost absurd immensity, each one of us has a unique function to perform, a unique contribution to make. Within the billions of planets orbiting billions of stars, within billions of galaxies *no one can fill our shoes.* Without our individual contribution—the world is incomplete, wanting. It is as much as to say that that which is perfect must discover and recognize its own perfection before it can do justice to its existence. To do so, we must reach beyond the limitations of our bodies, our minds, and link up with the transcendent, with that which is beyond words, logic, mental concepts or imagination. We must, as the Sufi poet Rumi said, reach out beyond the realm of doing right and doing wrong. There, and only there, we find our *dharma*, our destiny, not only in the esoteric sense, but as it applies to our everyday life. Once we discover the purpose for our existence, we shall enter and remain in a state of bliss—as long as we adhere to it in total commitment, in total abandon.

Such is the power of dharma. Such is our destiny.

Most people I've met over the years seem to tread water, resigned to what they believe to be their taxing lot. They perform their duties with little or no enthusiasm. They justify their somber existence with utterances regarding their sense of duty, obligations, real or assumed. To justify their misery they cite a demanding wife, a bunch of children, aging parents, assumed commitments, loyalty, demands of their religions, national traditions, and even their moral obligation to keep up with the Joneses, the Does, the Smiths. While such a stance is indeed fully justified by the prevailing social standards, it does not do justice to their true potential. They live in irons of their own making. They suffer. Really suffer.

In worst cases, they suffer indifference.

An ancient seer laid claim that we have been created in the image of God.(1) Unfortunately, the sage failed to describe the attributes of this deity, other than to affirm His power over us. Power to reward and/or punish the deserving. Later, the followers of this ancient creed invariably associated this "likeness" with a mystical yet strangely anthropomorphic imagery. The gods were larger-than-life paradigms, paragons of virtue, models for all humans to emulate yet never reach. Those ancient gods resided in heaven, awaiting us to join them in the fullness of time.

Yet such gods do not exist.

There never had been such gods.

God has no being except in a mode of being.(2) There is no existence without form. Without form there is only a possibility, a potential. Perhaps even *Infinite Potential*. This Potential translates Itself into Prime Cause. Anything already created is the result of a cause. Prime Cause precedes the universe. In IT'S likeness we have been created. We are the Prime Cause of the universes in which we have our being. We create our likes and dislikes, our wealth and our poverty, our happiness and our misery. In the illusion of our material bodies we observe the consequences of our creative endeavors.

Yet, in the material sense of the word, we do not exist.

We are detached observers, spectators, shifting our attention among the milliard possible options, which, when directed by our attention and desire, come into material existence. The very word guides us towards the truth: existence, from Latin *existere*, means *coming forth*. An emerging from a potential possibility into an actual, if ephemeral, form. Thus our material body, our physical presence, is not our true nature. Our material presence is no more than the *result* of the intercourse between our mind and the Field of Infinite Possibilities.

We are gods, indeed!

So what of *dharma*? It is little more that a memory of a dream.

We conjure up our lives, our experiences to suit our needs for learning. We create conditions in which we can contribute most to the universe. Then, we try to match our deeds with our dreams. When we succeed, we experience bliss.

So if anyone does not abide in a state of bliss, they have only themselves to blame. It is up to us to discover our individual purpose. We must remember. We must remember who we are, and why are we are here. If we adopt just these two tenets we shall have made a giant step towards the state of bliss. After all, heaven is within us. Heaven, the Field of Infinite Potential, is waiting to be discovered. We must discard life of fear. We must stop all struggle, deny the necessity of suffering, dismiss battles for "survival". After all, the level of our evolution is directly proportional to our understanding of our true nature. We must remember that at a very primordial level we never left Eden. Now and again we embark on a short journey. It is up to us if the journey is one of bliss.

***
981126

FOOTNOTES

1. In Genesis 1:27 The English translation states: So god created man in his (own) image. The word "god" is taken from the Hebrew *elohim*, which means gods (plural), or objects of worship.
2. Compare: God has no other being than a "being as something". EXPLORING THE CRACK IN THE COSMIC EGG, Washington Square Press, 1975].

Where there is faith, there is love.
Where there is love, there is peace.
Where there is peace, there is truth.
Where there is truth, there is God.
Where there is God, there is Bliss.

Sai Baba

44
SPIRITUAL LIFE

Only three more flights...
Her knees began bleeding on the forty-fourth step. Every Good Friday—always on the forty-fourth step... The steps used to be lined with a coarse carpet. Now the church can no longer afford one. It's really hard on the knees.
Only one more flight.
The agony in her knees is so great sister Angelica is slipping into a trance. Ah, the wonderful pain... Humbly, she lifts her eyes to the crucifix atop the St. Joseph's. It seems enveloped within a strange light. An aura. Her heart is filled with great joy. Perhaps this year she'll make it to the top... Perhaps she will feel...
The arms of her Savior reach out and lift her just before she faints. She wakes up in the local clinic. The Savior is nowhere to be seen. Only the pain remains.

Sister Angelica does the penitential pilgrimage every year. She must. There is so much sin in the world. So much evil. What else can she do? She gave herself to spiritual life, oh, so long ago. Climbing the hard steps on her knees has been relatively easy—when she was young. Now? Now nothing is easy. But she must keep trying. Last year she almost felt Christ's arms around her waist. Just before she fell.

***

There are those, reportedly the Pope among them, who wear haircloth. Not many, nowadays. Some still pierce their bodies, ears eyebrows, noses, tongues, nipples, but those are mostly youth in need of recognition. Some still indulge in flagellation. Not monks, not aspiring saints, but frustrated businessmen seeking outlet for their sexual inadequacies. Some believe that their voluntary suffering will ease the pain in Christ's crown of thorns implanted by our sins 2000 years ago. Others just like the pain. It is an escape from a reality they cannot face. It gives them an illusion of pleasure, an emotional outlet, often assisted by hard drugs. They know no other pleasure. They are lost. The psychiatric wards can do little to help them. The good doctors no longer pretend, like their sacerdotal predecessors, that physical pain, self-denial, mortification will lead their patients to heaven. Perhaps they lost the road map. Perhaps they've just outgrown some of the perversions of the human mind.

***

Today is Thursday. Sister Angelica feels better. She stopped having nightmares. She'll be all right.

Until the next year.

***

What is spiritual life?

These things I have spoken unto you, that my joy might remain in you, and that your joy might be full (John 15:11). So said a man in whose name thousands abused, and continue to abuse, their bodies with penitent practices that would make Marquise de Sade proud. Yet among These things there is no mention of discomforts of haircloth underwear, of fasting, flagellation, mortification, immolation, self-induced punishment, or any other form of aberrant practices. Of any form of obscure escapism from the fullness of life.

No mention of climbing hundreds of steps on your bare knees.

If our life is not filled with joy—we are not Christians. If we do not delight daily in the "good news"—we are not

Christians. If we think of ourselves as sinners rather than children of the Most High—we are not Christians.

If we do not love one another—we are not Christians.

Wherever there is strife, discord, conflict, contention, disharmony, dissension, disunity, division, mischief, war—there is no love. Wherever there is suffering, distress, misery, affliction, anguish, grief, heartbreak, sorrow, woe, pain, denial, sadness, indifference, there no love—nor is there faith, nor abundant hope. Whenever we do not rejoice in life, there is no love—because joy is the amalgam of Life and Love.

Spiritual life is living in the fullness of life.

It is being aware of the abundance of gifts that are ours to enjoy. It is finding joy where others see sorrow. It is finding love where others feel hatred. It is forgiving when others yearn for revenge. It is offering warmth and compassion when others offer indifference. Spiritual life is finding good in everything, everywhere, at all times—because evil is an illusion.

For me, it is also walking the middle path, rejecting extremes, observing, learning, sharing, accepting everyone on my journey as extensions of my own being. It is losing the distinction between you and me. It is sensing oneness with all creation. It is living in full consciousness.

It is accepting full responsibility for my thoughts, words, emotions and actions.

It is never escaping from life, it is finding it.

It is embracing my own immortality.

It is living in the present.

***

981128

45
THE FINAL VICTORY

A biographical essay written four days before my father's death.
My father has not spoken for more than two years.

It took quite a while. When Alzheimer first stretched its tentacles to affect my reasoning powers, I dismissed it as just another name for growing old. Let them say what they will—I said to myself—I'll stick it out for as long as I can. It made sense, at the time. Life in my aging body was the only life I've been aware of for more than ninety-years. That's quite a time to get used to it. My body, I mean. My body, my brain, my memory cells, all those bits and pieces, which we, humans, recognize as ourselves. Which I recognized as "I".

But then things got worse. At first it seemed only an exacerbation of what I already recognized as aging. But when my hearing gave up on me, I was forced to turn my attention inward. It's quite simple really; when you lose contact with the outside world, your inner senses compensate. My dreams became longer, more complex, richer in subject matter, in texture. The colors I've seen were more intense, my sensations more acute, my involvement more penetrating. In some dreams I actually controlled their course. I was the observer and the observed.

The dreams, too real to be called dreams, really, fascinated me.

Sadly, when I awoke, I could see in the eyes of the staff tending to my body, that they thought that I suffered. Nothing could have been further from the truth. Sure, I had some discomfort in my inability to clear my throat, my cough was nagging my bronchial tube, but, after all, what do you expect after over seventy years of regular smoking. Most people died long before my present years after smoking a lot less. I never considered minor discomfort as suffering, anyway. I cooked my goose; I was willing to eat it. I strongly suspect that the carbon monoxide in the cigarettes had a cumulative effect not only on my lungs but also on my brain-cells. That, in turn, affected my power of speech. My mind continued to function perfectly—it was my brain that got damaged. In fact, even as my brain refused to sustain intimate contact with the outside world, my mind continued to discover new vistas, new realms, new experiences. The nice people around me attempted to keep me awake for as long as possible; to keep me interested in the banalities of their reality. They were really kind people, but they had no idea of what marvelous experiences they were depriving me of. I have been willing enough to take part in physical activities, but they shackled me.

After my hip operation, I succeeded in climbing out of my bed over the high metal rails they have in hospitals and now, apparently, in institutes for senior citizens. But, no mere iron bars can imprison a cavalry officer. I climbed over them and went for a walk. And you know how they rewarded me? They tied me down. For my own good, of course; or rather for the good of my body. It might hurt itself. The old bones might crack, they said. So what if they did? I was willing to pay the price—after all, it was *my* body—what was left of it.

The kind nurses, and smiling sisters in angelic white gowns, seemed completely unaware that by depriving my body of activity, they were driving me into the only realm, which was not polluted by their doting kindness. Sure, I might have broken my legs, hips, neck or whatever—if I gallivanted at snails-pace along the hygienic corridors of the Institute, but so what? No one ever explained to me what were they saving my body for. They seemed to think that I am my body. It was as though they really thought that the real me is the decrepit 95 year old bag of bones and water. The amazing thing is that they were all religious people! Haven't they ever heard about soul? Haven't they heard that in my soul I am free? My wife knew, but she, like myself, was helpless. The doctors, nurses, sisters and all the trained staff constituted an overwhelming majority. They all cared deeply about my body—they ignored *me*. It was as though I didn't exist.

So there I was. Deprived of hearing, deprived of my power of speech, tied down to bed or a wheel-chair. Looking at TV gave little comfort. I couldn't hear what was said and my eyes weren't getting any better. Give me a break, I was 98 years old!

How time flies…

But it was too early to throw in the towel. I developed a new hobby to amuse my dilapidating body. I began eating like a horse. I ate full breakfast, full lunch, full supper and any snacks between the meals they cared to offer me. I've never refused a cake or a bit of chocolate. I would have eaten everything else in sight, but I lost all my teeth! For a while it was fun. Being completely stationary, I didn't burn any calories. And since I was tied down, they had to take care of the half-digested evacuation. Serves them right, poor sods. Yet, by bread alone a man liveth not. I kept it up for as long as I could but—enough is enough. Let them satisfy their need for kindness on somebody else. As for me, I decided to enter the realm of the vivid dreams—permanently.

You would have thought it would be easy.

Since for the last two years the only thing, which kept my body alive, was using it as a food-processing machine, all I had to do was to stop eating. By the way, by now I was over a hundred. *Over a 100 years old!* I think I was old enough to make my own decisions! Of course, I had no way of telling them that I was getting out. No power of speech, remember? In fact my brain was on the blink. I couldn't formulate a single sentence. There is an incredible gulf between one's mind and one's brain. Brain is like any other organ. If it doesn't function you can't use it.

So I've made my decision. My wife knew immediately what I wanted. For three days and nights I neither ate nor drank. I was really close to final release. And then....

... and then the good sisters, nurses and doctors stepped in. Since I didn't eat, they put me on intravenous feeding. Some people never give up on their need to be goody-goody. What really amazes me, though, is that those very same people, surely, believe in God, soul, and presumably some sort of "after life". Yet they seem to think that if I vacate my body, I'll die. Will they ever understand that it is my body which stopped functioning, not me? I've had a marvelous time for the last five years sleeping and dreaming for up to twenty hours a day. To hell with the body. I didn't need it any more. Sure it took me a long time to realize it, but now I know for certain that the real me has little to do with the body I occupy. Sure I used it for all it was worth. To learn, to mature, to share, to experience love. To saturate my awareness with joy. But now? The instrument doesn't work any more.

LET ME OUT OF HERE!
I cried. No one heard.

I got pretty desperate. The intravenous kept my body going. Only now I didn't move at all, got too week, and the old hulk was beginning to ache. I had to find a way out. Then I had it! With an enormous effort I mobilized the remnants of my physical responses and I began clotting the vein at the point of the needle. For a while they changed it from one arm to another. Then I served my *pièce de résistance*. I reduced my circulation so low they couldn't find the vein. They had to take me off the intravenous! I wish I could share the wonderful news with my wife, but I am sure she knew. We talked with our eyes every evening—for years and years...

My body is no longer tied down. I'm in no danger of climbing over the guardrail. Any moment now, I shall be free. Free in my soul.

Finally, I've won.

***
981221

One has to pay dearly for immortality;
one has to die several times while one is still alive.

Friedrich Wilhelm Nietzsche
[Philologist, philosopher, cultural critic, poet, composer]
1844 - 1900

When you arrive at the sea,
you do not talk of the tributary.

Hakim sanai
[The Walled Garden of Truth]

I am the Self, seated in the hearts of all creatures.
I am the beginning, the middle,
and the end of all beings.

BHAGAVAD-GITA

46
POINTS OF VIEW

For years I've regarded people as states of consciousness. This viewpoint is not strictly accurate, because we are not the states as such, but we enter them and identify with them in order to gain experience. Yesterday, I entertained an old friend who, at one time, infected me with an "all consuming desire" to search for my identity. He also affirmed that we all are little more than points of view.

By now, my conviction that Soul drinks life, or mode of being, by individualizing Itself into countless physical embodiments, is well known to the reader. To illustrate my thesis(1), each such embodiment represents a unique point of view, tempered or modulated by millions of successive incarnations, diverse experiences, distinct achievements. On a micro-scale, It is comparable to each cell in our physical body, each colored by its genetic code, each reporting to the central control, the brain, its sensory impressions. Through neural connectors the individual cell feeds our brain with impressions gathered by our senses. In the brain, the information is sorted, classified and stored for future use. At the mental level, such inputs contribute to, and create, our subconscious. The Bible calls this storehouse of information *nephesh*, (animal) soul, not to be confused with the Divine Presence, or the individualization of the one Soul.

Such individualizations, however, are inseparable and integral components of the Whole, to which each one of us contributes our individual point of view.

An architect sees the world from the point of view of an architect. He will not only judge buildings with a critical eye, but he is apt to apply similar parameters when regarding a woman. He will think of her as endowed with a fine (bone) structure, comment on her silhouette (front and rear elevations), admire her facade (skin, complexion). To a musician, the same woman might foster images of a beautiful sonata, an "appassionata", or perhaps a symphonic poem; to a woman—a handsome composer might conjure images of a "barcarole". A poet, perchance, might ask: "Shall I compare thee to a summer's day?"(2) To extend the analogy, while a doctor of medicine probably views us as complex biological structures, a nuclear scientists might think of us as void interspersed with countless atoms in a state of acute agitation.

There are as many points of view as there are individualizations of the Whole. Yet what matters, ultimately, is not how we define others, but how we regard ourselves.

To take full advantage of the available playground, we must accept two premises:
1. The universe has already been created, and
2. The human race is part of a secondary creative process only.

By the above I mean that the creation of the world is finished, and it is already extant in the form of innumerable states of consciousness. Our (human) creative process is limited to slipping into the various (extant) states and manifesting them in (or bringing them out into) the physical reality. We can learn enough about the workings of the world to enter the "ready made" states at our leisure. We can also choose to resist the inevitable flow of cosmic energies and become a battleground between our personal will, our ego, and that-which-is. The vast majority of the human race chooses the latter and suffers the inevitable consequences of ignorance.

But we do have a choice of scenarios. In this sense, we enjoy free will.

We can choose to regard the flow of the world's unfolding history as we would a fascinating film on our videos. Being observers we enjoy total detachment. Oh, we might, on occasion, get involved emotionally with the fate of the hero; we might even participate in mental acrobatics instigated by the playwright or the director. But, all along, we'd know that we are watching a film. This is exactly what we do as Soul. We watch and learn from the mistakes of the "body" we occupy.(3) As the world unfolds, our points of view unfold with it. We accumulate knowledge until such a time, as we shall create our own world and let it unfold.

We must never forget that Soul has Its being outside the constrains of time and space. It cannot participate directly in the affairs of the physical world except through Its temporary hosts. In order to gain experience of emotional states, It must assume, one might say "pretend to be", an astral (imaginative) body. The same is true of mental or physical experiences. From such vantage points It observes different reactions of Its host to the prearranged events (states of consciousness). Soul learns by becoming one (or embodying Itself) with the object of Its attention. It learns by direct perception. It does not mean that we should reject or abdicate the enjoyment, which the physical world provides. It only means that we must be aware that the material world is transient, held within the cosmic matrix of forces for only as long as we choose to remain in a given *state of consciousness*. It is our *attention*, which sustains it.

In other words, to iterate, the material world is not real.

The first step towards gaining control of the transient states is to realign our point of view. *Nothing else changes*. The world remains as "real" as it ever was, but we now regard it from a new vantage point. We place it in its proper perspective. We act the part of the host, but we do not, necessarily, identify with it. We give the very best performance we can, but we no longer confuse it with ultimate reality. We are no longer dependent on wiles, trials and tribulations of material, illusory scenarios. We become free agents, ready to change our point of view at will. This single realization sets us on the way to freedom. We take the first step towards becoming princes of our domain. We are on the way to becoming masters of our destiny.

The Mastership is not, and never could be, a state of stagnation. It is a state of *conscious* participation, of attainment, through a mode of being. The resultant joy of discovery is the never-ending reward. Heaven, the immense ocean of infinite potential, of infinite states of consciousness—
—ready and waiting—is ours to explore.

All we must do is change our vantage ground. As my friend mentioned, after we shed our bodies, our airs of importance, our moral indignation and puffed-up egos, we are little more than points of view.

***

990104

FOOTNOTES

1. I do not claim authorship of this assertion, but merely try to reinforce and illustrate from my own experience the conclusion reached by many people before me.
2. William Shakespeare, XVIII Sonnet
3. In this context, by "body" I mean the physical, emotional and mental construct.

47
A LITTLE BANG

To everything there is a season,
and a time to every purpose under the heaven:
A time to be born, and a time to die...(1)

According to the scientists, what holds true for man must also hold true for the universe. Both are born from a speck of dust—to a speck of dust shall they return. Yet if man and universe are cast in the same mould then, surely, the universes must be immortal even as man is immortal. Not in preserving the same form, but in being made from the same essence. Perhaps the universe is the image of God, even as we are. In the Koran it is written, "wherever you turn, there is the Face of God." Can God's face shrink and wither into a spec of dust?

Or are we and the universe the mode in which the Ineffable finds Its Being.

Over the years, I'd read various scientific papers that made no sense at all. They sounded like a dog running after its tail and complaining that the tail is escaping the grasp of his teeth. The problem is that the scientific community feeds upon its own excrement. Not the putrid variety, but on the sonorous regurgitation of their minds. Apparently, a scientist must publish. If they don't publish they wither and die—rather like the universes of their making. What they publish is of no consequence, providing they don't upset (too much) the status quo. No matter now fatuous, insensate, or out of date.

For as long as I can remember, I'd read, and heard, and continue hearing, about the primordial Big Bang. For some unknown reason the cosmologists insist on trying to retrace the universal birth to the first few billionth of a second. Yet they still can't decide whether the world will continue to expand forever, or collapse into another enigmatic Cosmic Egg, (or find a cure for a common cold!). Expansion and contraction, they call it. An oscillating universe. Rather like their theories.

If we were to take the Bible at all seriously, we might note that we, you and I, are created in the image of God. It might well suffice to study our own characteristics in order to learn about the universe. Alas, our illustrious astrophysicists, often proudly, assert profound ignorance of the Bible (or any esoteric writings).(2) Yet even a cursory glance at the incredible co-ordination and intricate interrelationships between the trillions of cells, let alone atoms, comprising a human body, might shed a lot of light on the workings of the universe. More importantly, if the Bible makes any sense at all, then the universe too must display a dual nature: the Cause and the Effect. The Potential and the Manifestation. The Immortal, Indestructible and the Transient, the Ephemeral—even if the Transient were to last a few aeons of our time. Can there be a coin with only one face?

It would seem ungodly.

Big Bangs, Little Bangs, Eternal Beginnings. Plural. Not one, single bang, but an endless procession of bangs, even as Fred Hoyle proposed way backs in 1948.(3) Even though, in the meantime, many suns, star systems and galaxies may die.

When a sun burns out part of its fuel, it eventually collapses under its own gravitational pressure to a tiny relic of its previous grandeur. In turn, the internal heat created by such a cataclysmic collapse is so great that the star often explodes. It goes Nova. Such final blasts of glory we could call Little Bangs. When a star starts with a much larger mass, it may explode with a much greater fury. Such stellar cataclysms are called Supernovae. Or: Much-Larger-Bangs. What is left of such stars after their annihilating expansions and subsequent shrinkages usually persists for countless aeons in the form of white dwarfs—aged, suns, the galactic senior citizens which have long finished their useful, productive lives.

There is one other collapse, even more enigmatic.

When the gravitational forces acting on the star's outer layers cross certain limits, the star continues to collapse, their protons and electrons are squashed into neutrons(4), then all subatomic spaces are compressed into what is known as degenerate matter. If the process doesn't stop there, the star shrinks into virtual non-existence, or what the physicists call, a Black Hole. An invisible dot with a gargantuan gravitational field so great that even photons cannot escape it.(5)

So much for intergalactic death.

A single galaxy, such as our Milky Way, can be the host of almost countless white dwarfs, neutron stars, and even black holes. The black holes have the additional power to collapse space itself. If our whole galaxy were to collapse into a Black Hole, our universe would have ended. All matter, all energy, and all space would shrink into a speck of dust. A Big Crunch.

So far all seems relatively (no pun intended) simple.

Until...

Until a gentleman named Alexander Vilenkin put on his thinking cap. Vilenkin is a faculty member of Tufts University who likes to play with cosmic ideas. While cosmology is not officially his specialty, his ideas shook the scientific establishment. Vilenkin began with the premise of quantum physics that the void of outer space is not void at all, but consists of an energy field whose random fluctuations allow for the formation of very tiny particles. [Remember Hole?] Usually the energy is insufficient to sustain the life of these particles and therefore they blink in and out of existence. In fact their lifespan is so short that they are called virtual particles. Where Vilenkin put a spanner into the astrophysical works is, with a seemingly simple question, that if particles can spring into life out of "nothing", why not a whole universe. And if a universe can spring into life out of nothing, why not many, many, in fact countless universes? Of course only those universes which could muster sufficient stamina from the vast concentrations of energy called "cosmic strings" would survive. Others would, sort of, wink out. Rather like thousands of ideas that cross our minds, but which we do not sustain with our attention.

By these standards the biblical model wherein God took a whole week to create the universe must seem like snail's pace. A virtual universe would inflate with space at rates vastly exceeding the velocity of light....

Frankly, none of this really matters. Not unless you are an astrophysicist and make your living by dreaming up improvable (if not improbable) theories. Unless you are a cosmological dreamer. For me it does not matter because I live in the present.

The Eternal Present.

So here we have Big, Middle-of-the-road, Little, and perhaps even just Virtual Bangs. What concerns me is that fantasies such as the string or the super-string theories(6), or the virtual particles, or bangs of any size, can never be subjected to an experiment. And there is only one criterion, which separates philosophy from science, and that is testability. We may not have, as yet, unified science and religion, but philosophy has long entrenched itself into scientific respectability.

Perhaps religions are next.

Naturally, orthodox religions based on outdated knowledge will run their course, and follow the way of the geocentric (as well as anthropocentric) Dinosauria. But new religions will encourage the search of the universe within our own hearts, within the Soul... such religions could well show us the Face of God reflected in the eternal, ever-changing, ever-expanding universe.

***
990927

FOOTNOTES

1. Ecclesiastes 3 :1-2
2. Albert Einstein is said to have kept of copy of H. Blavatsky's SECRET DOCTRINE on his bedside table. I suspect such deviations from scientific thought would be frowned on today.
3. In 1948 three astronomers, Hermann Bondi, Thomas Gold and Free Hoyle advanced the "continuous creation" or the "steady-state" theory, which proposed that hydrogen is being continually created out of nothing. Compare to the 1982 Alexander Vilenkins's version of the virtual particles.
4. This phase is called a "neutron star". Its density would be about 1,000,000,000,000,000, grammes per cubic centimeter, and would be far denser than any known white dwarf.
5. This is why they are black, of course. Steven Hawking does state, however, that according to the quantum theory, there must be emissions from the "empty" space immediately outside the Black Hole horizon. [Hawking, Stephen W., A BRIEF HISTORY OF TIME, Bantam Books, Toronto 1988. pg.104-105]
6. See the following essay on *Visibilium and Invisibilium Omnium*, # 48

Success or failure is your own making.
You decide your destiny.
The Lord has no share in it.

Sai Baba

Stars are born in darkness, and in secret, they form deep within clouds of interstellar gas and dust so dense and opaque that no visible light can escape, and so their births have been kept well hidden from our earthbound telescopes. Unable to pierce the black veil, astronomers have had to content themselves with constructing, from physical principles, their own scenarios for how a star takes shape.

Adam Frank
In the Nursery of the Stars
[DISCOVER, February 1996]

48
VISIBILIUM OMNIUM OR... 10%

The astrophysicists, the astronomers, probably all the scientists as well as at least 90% of the rest of us, are preoccupied with the visible universe. Yet those very same scientists assure us that no more than 10% of the world's matter is visible while 90% remains invisible. There is the "black matter", matter not emitting any light. There are trillions of dying stars—hoary "white dwarfs" within galaxies so far away that their light is totally dispersed before it reaches our tiny spec of dust, our Earth. There are black holes, large and small, which sport such intense gravitational fields that not even light can escape them. They are all part of the invisible world. And then there are powerful energies, and fields, and forces—weak and strong, all invisible to the human eye. We live within a universe of which at least 90% remains as elusive as God or Spirit is to a most ardent "disbeliever". And, on the top of all that both, the visible and the invisible, universes lie firmly within the domain of the temporal, the transient, the ephemeral.

The whole universe lies within the realm of Maya—the realm of illusion.

Perhaps this is why the Roman Church, which until the age of Enlightenment wielded by far the most powerful influence on the development of Western thought, took such a seemingly universal viewpoint. It proclaimed, in the lately-lamented Latin creed, its belief in the Creator of *visibilium omnium et invisiblium* without specifying which is which, or allowing for the Potential of the Divine to reach out for that which is not yet manifested in either the visible or the invisible spectrum. Nevertheless, having declared its act of faith, the Church promptly shut its eyes to both, the visible and the invisible, lest it might impinge on its infallible interpretation of the Holy Scriptures.

Belief to belief.

Some time ago I discussed the centrifugal and the centripetal forces.(1) The most powerful of these (if we are to take our scientists seriously), the Big Bang and the Big Crunch, display a correspondence to the esoteric attributes we normally assign to the divine. The Big Bang and the Big Crunch cannot be located anywhere in space or time for the simple reason that both fall beyond those temporal parameters. When the Big Crunch approaches its zenith, the space will so curve around the heart of the maga-black-hole that it will collapse upon itself. When space is also eliminated within a singularity(2), time, its other component, disappears also. What is left is that which the mystics might call God. It is the sum-total of all that was, all that is, and all that could ever be. The Three in One, past, present and future pause within a contemporaneous harmony.

While those are cosmological concepts, they apply to us, individual human beings. Humanity began approaching this understanding with the introduction of two theories. The first, which applies to the great outer spaces, is the General Theory of Relativity. It might be said to describe the vast matrix of creation, God—if you like, or at least the 10% of the universe (or 10% of the manifested God), which is visible to our senses. The second theory is that of the Quantum Mechanics. This deals with the "within", the inner, infinitely small dimensions of God. In a way, this theory attempts to describe the invisible. Perhaps, when we combine the two theories, we shall get an inkling as to how the universe works. The problem is that the Quantum Theory relies on the uncertainty principle: on the… unknown. Rather like on an aspect of God that is not-fully-manifested.

It could be that in order to combine the two theories we must reach inside that which is physically unattainable. We must attempt to enter a universe before it becomes manifested. Though this sounds impossible, the powers that be gave us an opportunity. They created potential universes. We cannot see them, we cannot (as yet) enter them, nevertheless they exist and they even affect the universe we live in. Those as-yet-unmanifested universes we call: Black Holes.

At present, the scientists think of the Black Holes only in terms of *collapsed*, degenerate matter. Perhaps, one day, they will think of these very same Black Holes as of Black Eggs. Cosmic Eggs destined to give birth to new universes.

Some years ago, theoretical physicists advanced a new hypothesis, which, presumably they hope, will take us in the direction of a Unified Field Theory; the single theory that combines the visible and the invisible. In late 1960s they started talking about the "string theory". We all know that atoms are very small. Much smaller are its component parts such as protons, neutrons or electrons, though these are massive when compared to quarks, gluons or neutrinos.(3) Yet, to imagine the size of a "string" we must picture an atom being the size of the sun. Then a "string" would be the size of an atom. I think of "strings" as bits of vibrating fragments of information. The String Theory postulates that everything in the wide universe of ours is composed of strings.

A mystic might call them Divine Intelligence— quantified.

For thousands of years we chose to divide mystical and scientific research into two, often opposing, often contradictory, forces. In 1980 the (American) National Academy of Sciences issued a statement that "Religion and science are separate and mutually exclusive realms of human thought whose presentation in the same context leads to misunderstanding of both scientific theory and religious belief." It is apparent that many religious leaders share this view. I would suggest that all sciences and all religions that subscribe to this thesis are equally as unlikely to discover the Truth. After all, truth is one, the ways of approaching it as diverse as the units of awareness populating this, and any other earth. What must ultimately underscore our search is an unquestionable commitment that regardless from which direction we approach—the final destination is but One.

The time is coming when science and religion shall merge into a single discipline. What will bring this about is the realization that the universe is the creation of our mind, not the other way round. What will change is our vocabulary, and our perception. The more open-minded we become the greater will be the marriage between the two forces. And make no mistake about this, science and religion are enormous forces. Between them they shape the creative capacity of our mind, and thus our reality. It is our mental struggle, which influences the way the universe works, even as the product of our efforts—in turn—affects the way we think. A self-perpetuating conundrum. Science limits its realm to that which is manifested, the religion to the presumed potential. Within their chosen orbits, both are compromised. One chooses to study the effect, the other limits itself to the idolization of the Cause, at arm's length, cautiously calling It a "mystery".

Within their chosen orbits, both are incomplete.

It could be said that when we stop thinking we enter the realm the visible and the invisible, all at once. We enter the realm of a black hole where all the laws of the manifested universe hover in timeless abeyance. We become open to the Infinite Potential affecting our stream of consciousness. Perhaps when the scientist stops formulating his deciduous theories and the religionist stops his dogmatic preaching, both will acquire the art of listening. Listening to the quiet voice within their hearts: a tiny black hole filled with absolute silence.

A tiny black hole—filled with Light.

***
990922

FOOTNOTES

1. BEYOND RELIGION, Volume I, *Parallel Evolution*, April 1997. [© 1997, Inhousepress 2001, Smashwords Edition 2010]
2. Black Holes are also called Singularities.
3. "A hundred billion neutrinos pass through each square centimeter of the Earth's cross-section each second, as though he Earth were not there". [Isaac Asimov, THE UNIVERSE, Pelican Book 1971 pg. 261.] Latest Internet data suggest that more than 50 trillion solar electron neutrinos pass through the human body every second.

*The universe is made mostly
of dark matter and dark energy,
and we don't know what either of them is.*

Saul Perlmutter

American astrophysicist
Nobel Prize in Physics, Albert Einstein Medal;
Harvard University;
University of California, Berkeley,

49
MIRROR

In my essay *"The Greatest Crime"*, I discussed the Christian concept, which stresses the divinity of Jesus. I pointed out that at no time had Jesus laid claims to divinity. Quite the contrary, he repeatedly denied such "accusations", pointing out his limitations and deferring all credit to his "Father" in heaven. If we dare to contradict the belief of some one billion Christians, perhaps we might also dare to question Jesus' own judgement in this matter. What if Jesus was wrong and the Christian churches right?

We start our lives as uncut, rough diamonds. Our precious potential is hidden within, waiting to be honed, polished through our efforts, through our knowledge and will. The potential within is, as are diamonds, the most precious jewel in the world. Once polished, we become tiny mirrors of the universe. Not just the visible universe, but also the Potential, the unlimited Wholeness. These precious jewels, seemingly unbeknownst to most of us, are our souls.

John, in his mystical writings, expressed this sentiment quite clearly. He affirmed that our inherent potential acts as light that points the way towards our ultimate goal of becoming mirrors of the True Reality.(1) We retain, nevertheless, free will to oppose the potential within us. Eventually we shall all return to our original Source, though we can delay this process for, literally, billions of years. We can maintain an obeisant attitude towards our physical nature, towards the illusion placed in our path, and treat it as true reality. I have pointed out in a number of essays that the Eastern concept of *Maya*, or the illusory nature of the visible/material universe, is no longer a metaphysical or a religious concept but a matter of fact, of hard science. What we perceive with our "unhoned" senses is not the true reality; it is what we imagine, or believe, our reality is. As we change our beliefs, our reality changes. Whether we know it or not, we always act as mirrors to the universe in which we have our being.

Furthermore, as we are each cast in an individual mould, each one of us presents a slightly different reflection of the universe. Some of us are wonderful mirrors, souls polished to offer a virtually perfect reflection of the universal attributes. These belong to great saints, saviors, mystics, occasionally poets. Most of us display some facets partially polished, giving some relatively true reflections, while our other facets remain obscured with shadows of illusion. Rather like partially polished diamonds—of noble material, but needing more love to bring them to their full potential. And then there are also those surfaces that show hardly any reflection at all. These are the self-absorbed aspects resulting from our egos, unable to look past the introverted reality of their own creation.

Unconditional love, when concentrated through the prism of a polished diamond, blazes with the light of a billion suns. Great souls reflect such splendor. To us, they shine as though with their own glory. But not so. They merely reflect the glory of the Whole. Of the True Reality. Of Truth.

Yet their reflections are so blinding that we cannot distinguish between the Reality and the perfect mirror. All we perceive is Light. We recognize it as God. And in a certain way, it is God.

A mystery? Confusion?

Not at all.

If God were a person He or She could insinuate Him/Herself into any being walking the Earth, or any other planet, and the host to such an event would be God indeed. Unfortunately for the Christians, as Jesus tried to explain, such a thing cannot happen. God is neither a person, nor a super-being, nor anything that could be limited to a singularity of expression. The very universality of the divine precludes such a possibility. Furthermore, God has no being other than in a mode of being. Such a mode of being we can find in Jesus, Buddha, saints and saviors... but also, if latent, in you and me. The whole universe is a divine mode of being. What differs is the degree to which the diamond of our soul is polished. Some of us reflect more of the true reality than others do. None of us can ever reflect the Whole. The Whole lies beyond the concepts of good and evil, beyond the fields of doing right and doing wrong, beyond any limitations or differentiation. By definition, the Whole is One. Nor can our mind embrace the concept of God, any more that we could embrace the whole universe with our arms. The light of such reality is so great that should any "mortal" attempt to reflect such glory before loosing his ego, he would be burned to a cinder. *Thou canst not see my face: for there shall no man see me, and live.*(2) Unless the facets of his soul were so polished that all the light would be reflected and dispersed throughout the universes. Unless he or she were a Perfect Mirror.

And if we were such beings, people would follow us and call us gods. It could hardly be otherwise. They would confuse the perfect reflection with that which it reflects.

And yet....
And yet WE ARE GODS.
No one can ever impose on us the reality of other universes. We and we alone are the builders, creators, sustainers and eventual destroyers of our realities. For us there is no god other than God within us. A promise of Infinite Potential. And *Thou shalt have no other gods before me.*(3)

And so it is.

Searching for God in a church or a temple is as futile as attempting to find Him anywhere outside our own being. It's not that God is absent from any particular location. God is omnipresent. Nor am I attempting to dissuade anyone from going to a church, a temple or any other place of worship. But if we cannot find Him within, how can we hope to find Him without? God is wherever you are. If you go to a church, He is there. If you wander into a desert, He is there.

If you keep very still, He is within the stillness of your heart.

***

990330

FOOTNOTES

1. "A lamp am I to you that perceive me—A mirror am I to you that know me." Apocryphal Acts of John.
2. Exodus 33:20
3. Exodus 20:3

"If I ascend up into heaven, thou art there:
if I make my bed in hell, behold, thou art there.
If I take the wings of the morning, and dwell in the uttermost
parts of the sea:
Even there shall thy hand lead me,
and thy right hand shall hold me."

Psalm
139: 8-10

50
THE DEVIL

"The devil made me do it!"

We create gods, we create devils. There is an inherent need within the human psyche that demands of us that we worship. People steeped in religion hate no one more than those who claim no allegiance to either a god or a devil.

"Oh, but, surely, you must believe in something..." is the unbelieving query rejecting the unbelief of others.

"Oh, I do, I do..."

The question is in what!?

"How about myself."

"That's pride speaking through you," accuse the believers.

(The believers like to accuse). "Well, didn't it say somewhere that we are created unto the image of God?"

"Yes...?"

(The believers hate to have scriptures quoted at them). "Well, why shouldn't I worship the *image* of God?"

"The Devil you should!!!"

"The devil I shouldn't?"

This could go on forever. Belief to belief. Myth to myth. Need to need.

A wonderful teacher, the late Emmet Fox, refused to accept the existence of the devil. To him, the devil was an invention of the human psyche, the human mind, brought about by the absence of light, or goodness, or God. The devil was not a "something". He was a no-thing. A void. A contradiction or denial of reality.

A different viewpoint will assert that the devil, or Satan, is any state of consciousness that recognizes anything other than the Spirit as True Reality. In the Bible, such a person is said to be demonized from the Greek *daimonizomai*, a verb, which our forefathers decided to transpose to a noun: the devil. The Greek *diabolos* meaning an accuser and/or calumniator (obviously a liar), which also signifies our lower nature, had been also, presumably for the sake of the contemporary primitive people, personified as "the devil". We must ever recall the powerful influence of the Greek culture which tended to personify, if not actually deify, all the human traits. Thus our lower nature became deified as the devil, which later religions tended to place on almost an equal footing with God. Ergo the dichotomy of the present-day Christianity and Islam wherein God is equally capable of infinite love, infinite mercy and infinite, cruel, unforgiving (eternal) punishment.

In the Old Testament the Hebrew word *sair* meaning: the hairy one, kid, or a goat, is twice translated as the devil, as is *shed* meaning spoiler or destroyer. The English word "devil" thus appears in the voluminous Old Testament a grand total of four times. No personified devils there, as there are no personified gods. The word Satan enjoys greater popularity though is practically limited to the book of Job in which he plays the part of the hater or the accuser.(1)

Thus the personification of evil is a later metaphysical invention, presumably designed to scare the believers into obedience and/or submission, in line with the "carrot and the stick" policy of training rather than educating people.(2)

People themselves, for their part, tend to create the devil in order to have someone or something to blame for their own shortcomings. Perhaps we forget that no matter how we improve our errant ways, perfection is not a goal but a signpost. No matter how many aeons we spend in countless reincarnations, we shall never achieve perfection. *"...there is none good but one, that is God"* Jesus assured us.(3) To Jesus, God and Good are synonymous. This attitude is not intended to disenchant the dilettante embryonic Mary Poppinses adorning our reality, but to offer them hope that no matter how "good" they become, there is always room for further improvement. This is the consequence of the very principle of immortality, which, in turn, entails continuity.

Some major religions assure their believers that this present life (I prefer to call it incarnation) is the only life they shall ever live. Depending on our abilities, after this ephemeral fraction of eternity, we shall be whisked off to an eternal consequence of our thoughts and deeds.

Half-truths are the most dangerous of all.

While it is true that our present life shall never precisely repeat itself, this is not due to the limitation of time but because *we do, in fact, enjoy but a single life*. A previous life (incarnation) can no more repeat itself than the previous day or the previous hour. Life has neither beginning nor end. Life is Life. Life IS. Soul neither was, nor will be. Soul IS. It is an individualization of that which IS. God IS and we are individualizations of God. As such we ARE.

And this is where the devil concept comes in. By accepting as reality that which is steeped in time and space we pay homage to illusion. Devil can be said to be the personification of this illusion that makes us think the material world as real. It is—in the same sense that Zeus, Hera, Aphrodite, Eros, Ares, Diana and countless other members of various pantheons of the past have been real. Every one of them has been spawned by our fertile imagination. We gave those gods reality by our belief. A transient reality is whatever we decide it is. If we manage to convince anyone that *our* reality is true, then the creation of our mind and senses becomes objective. If sufficient number of people believe in the existence of the devil, it, the personification of evil, becomes real. Very real.

But only to those who believe in such nonsense.

"Nonsense" means something that makes "no-sense". And for all who accept the concept of the omnipresence of God (Good), there is no room left for the "devil".

Furthermore, once we withdraw our belief in the reality of evil—the devil dissipates into the ether as did all other creations of our convoluted past. The gods are dead. We have outgrown them. There is only one True Reality, and that, we are assured, is not of this world.(4)

All else is illusion.

***

99100

FOOTNOTES

1. I tend to agree with the already mentioned Emmet Fox that the book of Job should be treated as a play, a drama, rather than an enigmatic philosophical dissertation.
2. See *The Carrot and the Stick (28)*, BEYOND RELIGION, Volume I. [Inhousepress, Montreal 1997, 2001, Smashwords Edition 2010]
3. Mark 10:18
4. John 18:36 et al.

"The Devil is the chief pillar of Faith. He is one of the grand personages whose life is closely allied to that of the church; ...if it was not for him, the Saviour, the Crucified, the Redeemer, would be but the most ridiculous of supernumeraries and the Cross an insult to good sense!"

Chevalier des Mousseaux

MOEURS ET PRATIQUES DES DEMONS, pg. x.

Des Mousseaux serves to illustrate the degree to which the Christians have been brainwashed. It should be remembered that, presumably for the reasons stated in the quotation, the Roman Church anathematized equally him who denied God and him who doubted the objective existence of Satan.

[Gleamed from H.P. Blavatsky, ISIS UNVEILED, Vol. I. Science. Theosophical University Press, California 1988, pg. 10300.]

51
THE UNDISCOVERED COUNTRY

"**Until death do us part...**" he and she swear at the altar. And then what? What about after death? Can I go and flirt to my heart's content? Most oath-givers do not wait that long. It seems that these-days the ceremony, or the rite, or the sacrament, of marriage is as meaningless as any other commitment regarding our behavior, in the context of relatively, if not completely, unknown and unpredictable circumstances.

Swear not at all... advises Jesus of Nazareth.(1)

He knew.

If you don't swear to start with, the question will not arise. I suggest that whatever happens twenty or thirty years down the road is as unknown as whatever happens after death. Making a commitment "until death" is not only absurd but also arrogant.

On the other hand to invoke death as a termination of *anything* is as irresponsible as it is futile. We simply do not know whether any change, whatever, occurs within our awareness at the precise moment our heart stops beating. Those who came close to such a juncture assure us that at no time did they lose their awareness of being.(2) We can only regard the future as the undiscovered county, as Columbus regarded what became known as America or the astronauts the outer space. As we grow older we seem to lose the capacity to reach out for the unknown. The familiar becomes dear to us. But for the young at heart, life is a stream, a current, a constant movement from the known to the unknown.

Although we regard death as the greatest unknown, it is hardly more so than, as mentioned above, whatever awaits us a few years down the road. Some attempt to predict the events in our many possible futures, ignoring earthquakes or other cataclysmic convulsions, ignoring the possibility of wars and riots, of military juntas, or other governmental fiascoes; ignoring unpredictable economical upheavals, environmental changes, viral or bacterial invasions, inexplicable plagues... Ignoring a thousand-and-one imponderables, including dangers inherent in crossing the street with or without "one belt too many" under one's belt. And all these are but the material, the physical aspects of our existence. What of mental and emotional upheavals? Are the effects of these not equally as unpredictable on our psyche, our mind and soul, as any of the other?

Future is an unknown—and this fact alone makes it fascinating.

Yet for some equally unknown reason people, most of us, attempt to predict the future, attempt to limit our horizons, to discipline them into mere mirrors of today. I am reminded a quip from a book I'd been given when I turned fifty: "I can finally afford all the things which no longer interest me." This truism is a lot less funny for all who forgot to live in the present—when they had their chance.

Life is defined by change. And the change always takes place in the present.

Always in the present.

And if our present life can be exemplified as change, what of later, after "death"? In Buddhist tradition, after we shed our physical bodies, we enter Bardo. And here we are stumped again. The word Bardo means... transition. While the transition refers to the period between successive reincarnations, the very word implies change. From a state of change we come, in change we shall continue. To experience the infinite possibilities which life offers, change is intrinsic. Stasis is the only death imaginable, and it can only happen to organizations, never to individual human beings.

Not once we come alive.

There are those who do not recognize our physical embodiment as life at all. *"Life is only the memory of a dream. It comes from no visible rain. It falls into no recognizable sea,"*(3) says Sai Baba, a man whom millions regard as the present incarnation of God. *"For in that sleep of death what dreams may come..."* wonders Hamlet.(4)

The concept of transition is not new. In the fifth century before our era, Socrates, with his dying words, left instructions to his friend Crito to offer a cock to Asclepius in gratitude for curing him from the pains and sorrows of this world. Asclepius was the Greek god of healing. Some five hundred years later, Jesus assured us that whosoever believes in him shall never die.(5) Sleep, perhaps, but never die. And yet, it seems to me, there are around a billion Christians who appear to be *very* afraid of death. They do not admit it, of course, but just look at them. They torture their bodies with countless chemicals, they undergo painful operations, transplantations, radiations... all to extend their sojourn in an aging, often dilapidating body. Do they really believe that they will never die?

Really?

There is no death.

There is only the Undiscovered Country. No man who became aware of his true identity can think of death as something finite, let alone final. Death is a form of transition as all other aspects of *life*. The vast majority of eschatological scholars are no more than atheists frightened by their own ignorance. Neither death, nor hell, nor heaven is final. They are little more than states of consciousness. Transient states of awareness. Only life is eternal and life is change. And change is the gathering of new experiences.

And sharing them. Sharing is loving. And love is the essence of immortality.

There is one truth that will set us all free from the fear of death: the discovery of who we are. Once we know that, there will be no more death in our scheme of things. It will never knock on our door. It will never scare us into acting like cowards. There is only change. And the Undiscovered Country.

***

991013

FOOTNOTES

1. Matthew 5:35
2. There is broad literature dealing with the so-called "near-death" experiences.
3. Schulman, Arnold BABA. [Simon & Shuster, Canada]
4. Shakespeare, William HAMLET, Act.3, Sc.1., [Courage Books, Philadelphia, London.]
5. John 11:26

*But that the dread of something after death,
the undiscover'd country from whose bourn
no traveller returns, puzzles the will
and makes us rather bear those ills we have
than fly to others that we know not of?
Thus conscience does make cowards of us all;*

William Shakespeare
[Hamlet, 3:1]

52
BEYOND RELIGION
II

As **man matured,** he began to travel.

In his early days, this man had to look after his own interests. Welfare state had not been invented. Insurance companies had not yet worked out their statistical data to determine the premiums he might have to pay in order to secure his own and his family's future. Outside his village, city, or national borders, he had been left on his own. Urban, later national organizations, had little influence outside their own boundaries. In time, the diplomatic posts offered some havens, but hardly enough to assure his wellbeing. In those early days of man's journeys, religions gave him a feeling of security, which only a sense of belonging to a large, powerful group can give. He began to feel comfortable in far away places with strange sounding names.

Religions knew no boundaries.

Whatever state could provide—religions provided much more. Wherever we went, regardless of the local political system, a Christian, a Moslem, a Jew, a practitioner of practically any religion, could find sanctuary in a church or a mosque, a temple or a synagogue, or whatever citadel a particular religion provided to its adherents. If we affirmed the same creed, we had been assured entry, succor and protection.

We became good actors. Regardless of our inner convictions, as long as we wore the outward masks of a specific religion, we could find haven in any port. Religious organizations offered unprecedented security.

And then new problems began.

Some churches grew so jealous of their expanding congregations, and the attendant economic benefits, that they fostered ill will towards other religions. Let us but glance at just three religions that preach the fundamental tenet of loving one's neighbor. Throughout the last millennium the Christians battled the Moslem and the Jews. The Moslem battled the Jews, who continue to battle the Moslem. The orthodox Jews began strife against their more tolerant brethren; the Catholics began murdering the Protestants who fought back with a truly Christian zeal. Not to be left behind, the Moslem extremists to this day slaughter any other Moslem who does not agree and conform to their idea of what being Moslem is all about. And this absurd farce has been, and continues to be, played out within the three powerful religions, which preach love for one's neighbor.

All three of them.(1)

What once contributed to our sense of security, now became a liability. Each religious group protected its priorities, the principal of which always was and still remains the survival of their particular church. This is what being orthodox is all about. "We" who are right versus "them" who are wrong. We shall be saved; the unbelievers shall fry in hell. There is no orthodox religion that preaches tolerance towards other religions at the expense of the scope of its own influence and interests.(2) Religious ideology is exploited to usurp power, to destroy and/or subject the opposition to one's will. A group-is-a-group, and in the eyes of its leaders, the "whole" is always more important than any of its parts.(3) "We might die, but our church shall survive!" The question at the expense of *which* "other" church never arises. It is always our church, our religion, and our faith. One item seems to have escaped and remains obscured to the leaders of all the orthodox religious assemblies. It is the fact is that we all belong to a very particular assembly, which heretofore escaped their notice.

We all belong to an assembly called the Human Race.

Exit religions.

In order to find commonality with the whole human race, we must be willing to forsake our allegiance to other, smaller affiliations. We must all become heretics.(4) We must reach beyond our traditions, beyond our personal likes and dislikes, beyond our inbred conditioning and look at the global village with fresh eyes. While politicians took the first steps towards the unification of the world through the creation of the League of Nations, later the United Nations, the World Bank, the International Red cross, and many other fledgling organizations, the churches, particularly the orthodox churches, appear to have remained in the darkness of the Middle Ages. To them, the points of individual dogmas are of far greater concern than the love for their neighbor. If they, all of them, do not change their "doctrines" to accommodate the inherent individually of man, we, the people, will have to take the next step on our own.

We shall have to step *BEYOND RELIGION*.

This in no way threatens our ethical or moral values. By stepping beyond religion we do not give up or forsake our faith. The original premises on which *all* the principal religions have been based—all lead to God. What varies is the definition of that deity as subsequently defined by the ensuing religions. In fact, if we are to believe that we are created in the image and likeness of God, if we are to believe Moses, Jesus or Mohammed (and all the great Avatars of the past and present), that we are all children of God, if we accept the premise that we must love one another—then religions have outlived their usefulness. By waiting any longer, we are apt to drift even further away from the original teaching. In time the theologians, theosophists, doctors of divinity (whatever that is), scholars bent of leaving their mark with some enigmatic interpretations of scriptures, will destroy the essence of the ancient teachings beyond recognition.

Stepping beyond religion means standing on one's own feet.

Once we do so, we shall become solely responsible for our salvation.(5) We shall no longer be able to lean on a learned rabbi, an imam, a humble priest from a local parish or the eminent vicar of Rome. We shall have to listen to the silent voice within. We shall have to learn to be silent in order to hear it. We shall make an enormous number of mistakes. We shall stumble, fall, get up—only to stumble again. But each time we lift ourselves from the gutter we shall be stronger, surer of our direction, more confident of the divine light showing us the way. And no matter how many errors we shall commit, not one of us shall organize the murderous wars, crusades, inquisitions, which our religions have sanctioned. Our mistakes shall be individual, not global. Perhaps we shall pay for our mistakes with our lives. But, after all, the religious leaders also paid for their mistakes with *our* lives for generations.

No more.

I shall leave you with this thought. According to the Torah which is the progenitor of the Jewish, Christian and Moslem religions, no church, no organization, no body politic, no sacerdotal fraternity has been created unto the image of God. You and I are.

Let us act accordingly.

***

991012

FOOTNOTES

1. Not to be left behind, the Hindus battle the Moslem, who battle the Shiites, who battle the Moslem, who battle the Hindus...

2. The word "orthodox" comes from Greek *orthos* meaning correct, and *doxa* meaning opinion (from *dokein* to think). Therefore adherents of any orthodox religion by definition assume all other religions to be wrong and therefore their followers subject to either conversion or elimination. While there

are tolerant people within most religious congregations, the sacerdotal helm rarely indulges in equal magnanimity.

3. See *Groups*, BEYOND RELIGION, Volume I. [© 1997, Inhousepress 2001]

4. The word heretic comes from Greek *haireticos* meaning: able to choose. A privilege which the orthodox religions deny us to this day.

5. see essay *Salvation*, BEYOND RELIGION, Volume I. [Inhousepress 2001, eBook 2009, Smashwords Edition 2010]

Never live without love, or you will be dead.
Die with love and you will remain alive.

Jalal-ud-Din-Rumi

Acknowledgments

I would be remiss were I not to thank my many friends for their comments, advice, and proofreading, none more so than Madeleine Witthoeft who's editing raised this book to acceptable literary standards. As always my gratitude to my wife, Bozena Happach, who put up with being a grass widow for weeks on end, and then offered me her inspired insights.

*Sincerely,
Stanisław Kapuściński*

ABOUT THE AUTHOR

Stanislaw Kapuscinski, (aka **Stan I.S. Law**) an architect, sculptor and writer was educated in Poland and England. Since 1965 he has resided in Canada. His special interests cover a broad spectrum of arts, sciences and philosophy. His fiction and non-fiction attest to his particular passion for the scope and the development of human potential. He authored more than thirty books, twenty of them novels.

Under his real name he published seven non-fiction books sharing his vision of reality. He also composed two collections of poems in his original native tongue in which he satirizes his view of the world while paying homage to Bozena Happach's sculptures.

BEYOND RELIGION III

Collected Essays

Stanislaw Kapuscinski
Inquiry into the Nature of Being
Volume Three

INHOUSEPRESS, MONTREAL, CANADA
http://inhousepress.ca

www.ingramcontent.com/pod-product-compliance
Lightning Source LLC
Chambersburg PA
CBHW061428040426
42450CB00007B/951